Praise for Mrs. T and
Chicken Soup for the Soul Presents Teens Talkin' Faith

"Chicken Soup for the Soul Presents Teens Talkin' Faith has given me new perspectives on life. It has helped me to realize that faith and hope, regardless of your circumstances, are not in vain. It let's you know that you are not alone. You are never alone."

—**Nick, 16**

"This book touched my heart and soul. Whether we doubt God or trust Him, these stories show us that God is near. I know that if other teens read this book, they will be as touched as I was. Thanks, Mrs. T, for showing me how to believe in life and depend on God."

—**Samantha, 14**

"A down to earth, truthful, and beautifully written book . . . It helped me realize just how wonderful God and life can be. It's the kind of book that will soon be tattered and dog-eared from being read again and again."

—**Reena, 14**

"As far as I am concerned, Mrs. T was sent here by God to share His love and compassion with us and to help us, as teens, to find our way. Thanks Mrs. T!"

—**David, 15**

"Every time I read Mrs. T's words or hear her speak, she reaches a place in my heart that I never knew I had."

—**Terran, 16**

Chicken Soup for the Soul®

TEENS TALKIN' PRESENTS FAITH

Jack Canfield
Mark Victor Hansen
Michelle L. Trujillo

HCI TEENS™

Health Communications, Inc.
Deerfield Beach, Florida

www.hcibooks.com
www.chickensoup.com

Library of Congress Cataloging-in-Publication Data
is available from the Library of Congress.

©2008 Jack T. Canfield and Hansen and Hansen LLC
ISBN-10: 0-7573-0733-7
ISBN-13: 978-0-7573-0733-1

Publisher: Health Communications, Inc.
            3201 S.W. 15th Street
            Deerfield Beach, FL 33442–8190

Cover photo Mariah L. Anderson
Cover design by Mariah L. Anderson
Interior book formatting by Lawna Patterson Oldfield

With love, this book is dedicated to you,
our teen readers. As teenagers, you are our future.
You have inspired us, taught us, and
challenged us to grow.

And to God, for His constant love
in our lives and His ever-present
encouragement that . . .

Now faith is being sure of what we hope for
and certain of what we do not see.

—HEBREWS 11:1

CONTENTS

ACKNOWLEDGMENTS

This book would not have become a reality without the input, insight, and inspiration of so many people. First and foremost, God! His presence joined us on the spiritual journey that became *Chicken Soup for the Soul Presents Teens Talkin' Faith*. We thank You and praise You, Lord, for Your inspiration and Your love. Through You, we know that all things are possible!

We would also like to thank our families:

Jack's family: Inga, Travis, Riley, Christopher, Oran, and Kyle, for all their love and support.

Mark's daughter, Elisabeth Del Gesso, and her son, Seth (Mark's grandson!), and Mark's daughter, Melanie Hansen, for once again sharing and lovingly supporting us in creating yet another book.

Michelle's husband, David, for his love, patience, and phenomenal editing skills . . . but mostly because he makes her life complete. To their children, Corey and Dani, for their teen wisdom and insight that helped this book to blossom into reality, and to her parents, Gary and Judy Williams, for being an incredible living example of faith day to day.

Our appreciation also goes out to:

Our publisher and friend, Peter Vegso, for his continuous support and allegiance to all of us and to the Chicken Soup brand.

Patty Aubery and Russ Kamalski, for being there on every step of the journey, with love, laughter, and endless creativity.

Barbara LoMonaco, for nourishing us with truly wonderful stories.

D'ette Corona, our coauthor liaison, who seamlessly manages twenty to thirty projects at a time. The time and energy you put into this book were a true blessing!

Patty Hansen, for her thorough and competent handling of the legal and licensing aspects of the *Chicken Soup for the Soul* books. You are magnificent at the challenge!

Michele Matrisciani, Carol Rosenberg, Andrea Gold, Allison Janse, and Katheline St. Fort, our editors at Health Communications, Inc., for their devotion to excellence.

Lori Golden, Kelly Maragni, Sean Geary, Patricia McConnell, Kim Weiss, Paola Fernandez-Rana, Christine Zambrano, and Jaron Hunter, for doing such an incredible job supporting our books.

Tom Sand, Claude Choquette, and Luc Jutras, who manage year after year to get our books transferred into thirty-six languages around the world.

Larissa Hise Henoch, Lawna Oldfield Patterson, and Andrea Perrine Brower, Justin Rotkowitz, Anthony Clausi, Peter Quintal, and Dawn Von Strolley Grove for their talent, creativity, and unrelenting patience while producing book covers and inside designs that capture the essence of Chicken Soup, and to Mariah Anderson for her creative artwork that made this cover so very unique. To Brandon, Hayley, Corey, and Dani, for making the jump on this cover, over and over again, literally!

Joe Gorton, Brandy Rapley, Laura Peterson, and the Rauber family: thank you for letting us share your stories.

And to Amanda, Sarah, Sion, Courtney, and Jason, too. We appreciate you all!

All of those who provided spiritual counsel, prayers, and scripture seeking, especially the pastors, priests, and youth leaders with whom we consulted: Judy Williams, Jaime Young, Phil and Velma Trujillo, Janell Sheets, Rosella Jordan, Joanne Kortan, Eileen Decker, and Callie Campbell Parr, as well as other friends and family who supported us throughout the process.

To Telsche Saunders, Amanda Dykes, and Father Warren Savage, who enthusiastically introduced the opportunity for their schools to be involved in this project. To every teen who submitted a story, we deeply appreciate your letting us into your lives and sharing your experiences with us. Thanks also to the many teachers and principals who allowed their students to write. For those whose stories were not chosen for publication, we hope the stories you are about to enjoy convey what was in your heart.

Because of the size of this project, we may have left out the names of some people who contributed along the way. If so, we are sorry, but please know that we really do appreciate you very much.

We are truly grateful and love you all!

A NOTE FROM JACK AND MARK

We are thrilled to present you with this new serving of *Chicken Soup for the Soul*.

When you open up *Chicken Soup for the Soul Presents Teens Talkin' Faith*, we hope that it will allow you to open your heart to discovering or renewing your faith. This book will offer an opportunity for you to accept, build, or strengthen your relationship with God. It is not a book about religion, but rather it is about teenagers expressing, exploring, and growing in their faith. This book is similar to our previous *Chicken Soup for the Teenage Soul* books in that we have compiled many writings from teenagers across the nation who will share with you their life experiences, from trial and tragedy to triumph and joy. They write from the heart about how God has given them strength and courage to deal with tough situations, along with love and comfort in times of loneliness or despair. They share what it means to accept God's grace and rely on His guidance. They also share stories of hope and joy. We have no doubt that you will relate to these teens as you read this book. We hope that their experiences and feelings will validate your own.

In addition, unlike our previous *Chicken Soup for the Teenage Soul* books, this one comes with an additional twist . . . and her name is Mrs. T. Actually, she is Michelle Trujillo, an author, speaker, and teacher, but her students and readers call her Mrs. T. She is known for her ability to listen without judgment and to share guidance with teens with humor and conviction to help them make healthy decisions. Like the teens who have written for this book, Mrs. T also writes from her heart. We believe that in doing so, she will touch yours. At the beginning and end of each chapter, she will share stories, insight, and life lessons in a section that we call "T" Talk. While reading these sections, it is our hope that you will be encouraged, challenged, and inspired.

We pray that you enjoy this book as you grow in your faith. May God bless you and keep you!

Jack Canfield and *Mark Victor Hansen*

A NOTE FROM MRS. T

While writing this book, I tried to put myself in your shoes. I realized that you may be incredibly strong in your faith and committed to God. On the other hand, you may be struggling with your spiritual beliefs and looking for answers. Perhaps you are not a Christian, but open to learning about God. Regardless, I pray that wherever you are on your spiritual journey, you will keep an open mind and allow the words written on these pages to touch your heart. My personal contributions are written from a Christian perspective. However, teens throughout the nation from all ethnic, socioeconomic, and religious backgrounds also contributed. Although I honor each contribution, it is important for you to know that the thoughts and beliefs of these teens do not directly reflect my thoughts and beliefs as the author. They also may not coincide with your personal ideas or opinions. So, please, take them for the individual life experiences and spiritual perspectives they are. In addition, please know that we have changed all of the names of the teen contributors, as well as a few of their ages, to protect their privacy and that of their friends and family. When needed, context and, less frequently, content were modified for the protection of those involved and to contribute to the continuity of each chapter.

The format of this book was designed with the input of teens like you. Each chapter of this book begins with an introduction or brief excerpt from me, Mrs. T, as I am known to most teens. This is followed by a collection of writings from teen contributors. Every chapter concludes with a "T" Talk, again written by me. I use the "T" Talks to summarize each chapter with personal stories, spiritual insight, and inspirational guidance.

Finally, know that Jack, Mark, and I wrote *Chicken Soup for the Soul Presents Teens Talkin' Faith* to honor God and bring His hope to you as a teenager. I pray that this book will lead you on a spiritual journey that will enrich your faith and draw you closer to God.

Mrs. T

Chapter One

FAITH!

JUST FOR STARTERS, LET'S TALK ABOUT FAITH . . .

At fifteen, Brandy was presumably a lot like you or some of your friends. She was a star athlete and incredibly social. Brandy hung with the "in" crowd and didn't have many worries. Her world revolved around school, friends, sports, and occasional parties. It was after one such party that Brandy's world was shattered. On the way home from this party, the truck she was riding in was hit by another vehicle and rolled three times. Ironically, out of the five people involved in the accident, Brandy was the only one badly injured and the only one not drinking that night. Brandy was left unconscious in the cab of the pickup while the others escaped to safety. Unaware that the truck would ignite, her friends were more concerned about staying out of trouble than rescuing Brandy. They either left the scene or scurried about trying to hide all evidence of their underage drinking. While they were scattering beer cans, Brandy was burning.

More than 75 percent of Brandy's body and most of her face were burned before a brave young man pulled her free from the hot flames. She lost her soft, smooth skin and her pretty hair. She lost her right ear, a finger on her right hand, and her entire left arm. Brandy lost her spot on the all-star softball team and her "normal" teen life of flirting with guys and hanging with friends.

In an instant, Brandy's life as a teenager changed. For many teens, appearance is extremely important. Acceptance is paramount. How teens look, dress, or what they are involved in can often determine their sense of belonging among their peers. Think about yourself. Are your looks important to you? Do you play any sports or a musical instrument? Are you involved in any clubs or after-school activities? Considering your life, can you imagine stepping into Brandy's shoes? Picture yourself so badly disfigured that you are no longer recognizable. Contemplate the changes you would have to make in your day-to-day activities if you lost one of your arms. Suppose you were the one left in that burning truck. Could you survive the pain, isolation, and extreme change? Would you even want to?

When I heard about Brandy, my initial response was to whisper to God, "Why . . . why did this have to happen? How can one girl go through so much?" But Brandy is able to see beyond my prevailing questions. Her faith has made her strong. A few years after her accident, Brandy and I became friends. The first time we spoke, she told me that she thanked God for her life today. She also astounded me with her wisdom when she said, "I don't blame God. Really, if I blame anyone, I blame myself because I was there. I chose to go to the party. I knew that the driver of the truck

I was riding in had been drinking, and I chose to put myself in that situation." However, Brandy understands that placing blame on herself, God, or the others involved in the accident has no benefit. So, instead, she acknowledges with gratefulness that she has evolved as a person and that her life has significant purpose. Yet that realization is not one that she came to readily. It was a slow awakening.

Five months after the accident and two days before her sixteenth birthday, Brandy was released from the hospital. Once home, she wanted to hang with friends and be a "regular" teen again. Although Brandy physically looked like a different person, inside she was still the same. This was very painful for Brandy because even her friends felt awkward initially. Like so many other people, they stared. So, when she went out with friends, she made decisions to drink and to be sexually promiscuous. Brandy struggled with the reasons why she made these choices, especially after all she had been through. Yet, she tested herself and her faith because she wanted to be "in." She wanted to be accepted.

Eventually, Brandy came to realize that many of the decisions she made after the accident were an attempt to prove to herself and her friends that nothing had changed and that she was still the same person. However, each time she participated in risky behavior, she knew it wasn't right. Slowly, Brandy grasped the notion that she didn't want to be the person she was before her accident. She realized that she used to be snobby, sometimes even rude to people. Her relationship with her mother was tense and argumentative. They didn't get along or do much together. At the time, Brandy felt that appearance was important and faith was insignificant. But Brandy grew to care more about people. She began to appreciate her mom, and they became closer than ever. She also came to understand that looks, in fact, don't matter. Instead, she learned that it is who you are inside that truly counts. Brandy began to cherish her relationships and value her faith.

As she looked back, Brandy realized the constants in her life were her family, close friends, and faith. Furthermore, she began to see that her faith, a treasure she often overlooked, was the strength that pulled her through. From the very beginning, when Brandy arrived by care flight at the hospital with her skin melted and charred, her mom asked her, "Is God with you?" Although she was really "out of it" and couldn't talk, Brandy nodded her head, "Yes, God is here." And even before that, as she lay in the midst of flames, a young man named Jimmy attempted to pull her free, but she was stuck in the cab of the truck. He tried and tried until he didn't think he could pull anymore, but God was there. In a final effort, with a silent prayer for help, Jimmy says that Brandy floated out of that truck as light as a feather. And following her recovery, Brandy knows that God was with her when she made poor decisions by helping her ultimately to choose the right paths. Brandy believes that if you ask God for help, He will help you. Through right or wrong, trial or suffering, He is there.

Throughout this book, you will find God's presence. Within these pages, as teens share their confusion and doubts, struggles and fears, triumphs and hopes, they will also share their faith. Regardless of where you reside spiritually at this point in your life, I pray that when you read this book, you allow God to embrace your heart.

Teens Talkin' Faith will lead you to discover unconditional love and help you to find peace in your life. It is a journey of faith toward God that will lead you to this discovery. If you are already strong in your spiritual or religious convictions, then you may know what I am talking about. Perhaps you have experienced the feeling of peace that enters your life when you turn to God for guidance or solace. Likely, you have felt the joy that fills your heart when you focus on the Lord. You don't need drugs, alcohol, or sex to find happiness as a teenager. You can find it in God. However, I'm sure that you know there is always room for spiritual growth.

On the other hand, if faith has never been a part of your life, then I am very excited to share the glory of God with you. My message in this book is enthusiastically simple. God cares! You can flee to Him for comfort. You can rely on Him for unconditional love. I want you to know that God is available and waiting for you to call on Him. He is there to guide, support, and, as He did for Brandy, provide courage and strength. His patience is plentiful, and His forgiveness is given freely. As a teen, you may experience small traumas in your life or painful tragedies like Brandy's. You may feel, sometimes, that you are all alone. But you are not. God is always there. Often, it is just a matter of opening your heart to His presence.

When you invite God into your life, His spirit will fill your heart. He is not a God who reigns from heaven demanding perfection and punishing anything less. Instead, He is someone with whom you can have a relationship. He is a God who loves you completely, with all of your faults and insecurities. You can talk to Him every day, every moment, because He always has time. God also inspired an awesome book that you can turn to for guidance and direction. It is the Bible, and it was written for you to foster your relationship with Him and help you to live a life full of joy and hope.

You might be thinking, Yeah, that sounds great, but how do I know God is really there? The answer is faith. What is faith? Faith is believing without actually seeing. It is relying on your heart instead of your head. Faith is letting go of the tough stuff in your life and turning it over to God, looking to Him for guidance and direction. Amazingly, faith is knowing in the depths of your soul that you are God's child and that He will take care of you.

Many teen contributors expressed that their faith grew by writing for this book. I hope that by reading this book your faith will grow, too. Like Brandy, you may experience trials or hardships in your life, but faith can help you to persevere. Brandy said that after her accident, she never wanted to give up. "I got a second chance," she said. "I am not going to sit here and waste what God has given me. I kind of feel like it was meant to be this way, like I am here for a reason." Her faith touched my life. Her wisdom opened my eyes. People often assume that you must be an adult to be wise. But after meeting Brandy and so many other teenagers, I know this isn't always the case. Wisdom can be born from experience. The teens who have written for this book share their experiences, doubts, wisdom, and faith with you. I hope that you consider them your friends. Appreciate their experiences and take from each something that you can apply to your life. Find love, faith, and hope on these pages. Find the Lord!

Mrs. T

. . . I BELIEVE GOD LOVES THE WHOLE ME . . .

When everything shifts in the maelstrom of my life, God is there, never-changing. My faith is very important to me because it is one of the only things that can never be taken from me. God is sticking with me, no matter how isolated or unpopular I get. Faith in God gives me more mental self-esteem. I believe God loves the whole me, both the good and the bad. That in itself is pretty cool. My faith is the perfect fit for me, and I know that as I grow, my faith will grow and change with me.

ROMELLE, 14

. . . I BELIEVE IN GOD
BECAUSE I NEED SOMETHING
TO BELIEVE IN . . .

For me, being a teenage kid living in this crazy, fast-paced world today, it gets confusing at times, and I need some solid ground. I find that in my faith in God.

Nobody really knows if God is real or not because not one of us has been to heaven and back, but I believe in God. I think it is important to have faith because without it, what is the point of living a life that leads to nothing? There has to be something more. I believe in God because I need something to believe in, and when I read the Bible, God is my answer. I believe because when I feel like nobody loves me and I am all alone in this world, I know there is someone with incomprehensible love for me no matter what. I know that I am never alone with God watching over me.

In times when I have been frightened or scared, I looked to God and felt better. He is the light when you are in the dark. I've been through some really rough times when I thought no one cared and everyone was leaving me, but

God was always there. Because of Him, I got through them.
God is comfort even during the worst times, and God
loves me no matter what I say or do. He is still there and
always loves me. That is why I believe in God, and that is
why my faith is important to me.

DANIEL, 14

I LOOK AT ALL
OF THE MIRACLES . . .

As I take a look around, up, and down and at all that surrounds me, I wonder.

I see people walking by, all different kinds. Trees and green grass growing and blowing in the wind, along with playful children who still hold their innocence, and I wonder.

I look to the old, grinning man—stories bundled up within him, so many years and experiences he must have. I look down to see all ten of my fingers that work and move, so many things that I can do. I look at all of the miracles around me, and I can't help but wonder, how can there be no God?

For it is moments like these, with peace and serenity, that God must be there, in this beautiful world that we live in, for all to share.

JENI, 14

I STARTED CHEMOTHERAPY
TREATMENTS . . .

Imagine feeling like you have your whole life before you only to find out you are about to face your second bout with leukemia. You are finally entering middle school, making plans for the future, eyeing the cute guys, talking about next week's game, and then the news comes . . . your cancer may have returned.

My first encounter with the disease came when I was in first grade. I became tired all the time and never felt like playing with the other children. Sitting on the teacher's lap or resting were the highlights of my recess. Then one day my temperature shot up, and the teacher contacted my parents who took me to the doctor immediately. Blood results revealed the diagnosis—acute lymphocitic leukemia. I started chemotherapy treatments that lasted for the next two-and-a-half years. Following that, I stayed in remission for almost three years. But then I relapsed at the start of my sixth-grade year.

This time was more difficult because I was older. I knew more of what to expect. I thought about my future, and I didn't want to die. I had peers who would make fun of me once they learned I had cancer. I am not sure they understood the seriousness of my disease, but their taunts added to my pain.

I started another series of chemotherapy treatments. My family and I were at a turning point with the disease. We had to decide if I would have a bone-marrow transplant or continue the treatment method I was presently receiving. I was fearful of having the transplant because I had known other patients who did not make it after their transplant. But it also helped some people get better. The deciding factor for me was when we found out my three-year-old brother was a perfect match.

I still had concerns because I consider my little brother "my miracle" from God, and I didn't want him to suffer. One day, while my brother was watching one of his favorite programs, I asked him if he would like to be a hero. He asked me, "Do you mean like Superman?" and I told him "even more than Superman." I explained to him that he would be saving his sissy's life, but it would require him to go through some pain and give lots of blood. At first, he told me, "No, I don't want to do that," so I was not going to press the issue with him. He turned back and started watching the television, but then about five minutes later, he turned and looked at me and said, "Sissy, I don't want to hurt, but if it will save your life, I will do it." Not only is he my miracle, he is my hero.

I left for the hospital and began preparations for my transplant the following day. I started with two weeks of testing to make sure I was in physical shape to begin the process followed by two weeks of radiation. Then, my brother and I went into surgery. Though it was tough for him, he responded very well and was out of the hospital soon. I stayed in the hospital for two months and then had to stay close by to make visits to the clinic daily, then every other day until finally decreasing to once a week.

This routine lasted for the next six months. At one point, it appeared I was relapsing because my white cells were not growing. I was required to take extra precautions like wearing a mask more often, staying out of public places, and—the hardest for me—not being able to have many visitors. My outings were limited to the apartment we were renting, the clinic, or a ride in our vehicle.

After six months, I was finally able to go home. I was welcomed by a parade of friends, family, and neighbors. It was such an exciting day for me and my family to finally be at home together. After the nine-month mark, I was able to do limited activities. Finally, after one year, my doctor allowed me to go out in public places. I still have certain limitations and will for some time to come. Doctor's visits are still a part of my life and will be for the next six years.

As you can tell, I have been through a lot, but I have never been upset or angry with God about my situation. I never wondered, "Why me?" but I did initially question what God's purpose was in all of this. Now I think I know. God has shown me that He is still in the miracle business, and He has allowed me to use my situation to witness to others about my faith and to minister to those who might be experiencing similar situations.

A verse that God gave me through this ordeal is John 11:4, which says, "This sickness will not end in death. No, it is for God's glory so that God's Son may be glorified through it." I truly want God glorified in my life. My favorite saying is "Keep your faith in God, and He will get you through it. He never leaves your side." My trust and faith in God have been my blanket of security through this experience and will continue to be what I cling to for my future.

HOPE, 14

. . . GOD PUSHES ME TO THRIVE . . .

The faith I have in God today

It keeps me strong in every way

I hold Him close

He keeps me safe

He lights my paths

When I have lost my way

My faith in God

It keeps me alive

My faith in God

Pushes me to thrive

My faith in God

It lets me know

I should never be afraid

Be afraid to show

Who I am

Or how life goes

My faith in God
It means so much
With every talk
With every touch
My faith is in God
I LOVE HIM SO MUCH

CRISS. 16

EVERYONE IS GOING TO HAVE A DIFFERENT REASON FOR BELIEVING . . .

One night, our youth group was having a lock-in where we spend the night at the church and usually have tons of fun. We were all excited about playing a new game called Romans and Christians. In this game, if you get caught by a Roman, you are sent to "jail" and asked the question, "Why do you believe in God?" When we played, and I got caught and the jail guard asked me, "Why do you believe in God?" I went totally blank. I couldn't answer. That night, I cried myself to sleep.

Why couldn't I come up with an answer? I have been a Christian all my life. I go to church every Sunday, pray regularly, go to youth group, and yet I didn't have an answer. Was it because I had only known this lifestyle because of my parents? And why did this question bother me so much? For the rest of the week, I thought and prayed about it. Then on Sunday night, as I was lying in bed, I found the answer.

In Psalm 27:1, it says, "The Lord is my light and my

salvation—whom shall I fear? The Lord is the stronghold of my life—of whom shall I be afraid?" This verse helped me determine why *I* believe in God. Without Him, I would have no salvation, no forgiveness, no afterlife, nothing. It is important to believe so I can have all of these things, and I don't have to wonder what will happen when I die. I know that I am going to heaven. If something bad or unexpected is bothering me, I can take it to God. Everyone is going to have a different reason for believing in God. I can say now that I believe in God because without Him I would be nothing and have no hope. Believing in God is a choice that everyone makes at some point. What is your choice; why do you believe?

KAILEY, 13

HE DIED IN A
FREAK ACCIDENT . . .

When I was only five, my big brother Ben protected me. I was in kindergarten, and he was in the seventh grade. He helped me cross the street after school each day. Traffic was very heavy on the way to the A&W root beer place. But we would go there, and Ben would treat me and our other brother to ice cream or french fries. When I was in the first grade and Ben was in the eighth, he showed me the ropes on the playground and held my hand when I was scared. None of the bullies messed with me when my brothers were around. In fact, up until I turned nine, they were my best and only friends. But then Ben taught me how to be "cool." He showed me all the right moves for becoming popular. He taught me to be more social and to work hard academically. By the time I was in the fifth grade, it was smooth sailing—straight As, tons of friends, and no worries.

That is, until four days before sixth grade started. On this day, I helped my family bury Ben's body on a hill that overlooked the pasture where we had ridden horses only the week before. He died in a freak accident just after he turned nineteen years old. Life as I knew it had changed. I turned to God. How could this crazy and horrible thing happen? Had I done something wrong so that I deserved to be punished? Ben was good and always helping other people. Why did God pick him to die? Would I ever stop being sad? Would my parents and brother ever be able to "come back" from this thing? These questions kept repeating in my head. I couldn't make sense of Ben's dying. I couldn't stop missing him. I hurt.

Then God began to give me answers. Almost a month after Ben died, my pastor was giving a sermon. He spoke about faith and trusting God to take care of every need, about letting God take control of our lives, about putting everything into His hands. He shared a verse from the gospel of Matthew: "Come to me when your burden is heavy, and I will give you rest." I somehow knew that this was true. And then he read to us from Phillippians 4:6–7. "Do not be anxious about anything, but in everything, by prayer and petition, with thanksgiving, present your requests to God. And the peace of God, which transcends all understanding, will guard your hearts and your minds in Christ Jesus." I was able to realize that when we give our sadness, confusion, and needs over to God, He takes care of everything. He has a plan and gives hope and a future to every person who asks and believes. There is nothing in all of life and death that God will not take care of if we allow Him to take control. As I thought about Ben, I realized that even if he wasn't there to hold my hand or teach me to be "cool," he had been there to help me find a deep and saving faith in God. He still protected me.

CLARK, 14

FAITH IS IMPORTANT TO ME BECAUSE . . .

I believe in God because I have no doubt in my mind that a higher power exists. When I look around me, there is so much goodness to be seen. Everything in the world had to have been created and planned ahead of time. As people, we do not simply appear on this Earth. Instead, God places each and every one of us here for a specific purpose. I personally feel God's presence around me in times of difficulty. He lends His hand in times when hope cannot be found. Faith is important to me because I feel that faith is necessary to build a healthy relationship with God. It is important to have something to believe in, for there is nothing greater than sharing in God's love. I have heard that if you do not believe in God during this life, and then you find that He truly does exist, you have everything to lose. If you do believe in God, and He does not exist, you have nothing to lose. And if you believe in God all of your life and He does exist, you have everything to gain. It is so evident that God does exist that there is no reason for me not to believe in Him. Faith in God helps enrich my soul. If I place all of my trust in God, I know that

He will always provide for me and lead me toward what is right and just.

DILLON, 18

I PRAY TO GOD EVERY NIGHT AND THANK HIM FOR MY LIFE . . .

I believe in God because He has helped me through my life. My mother is recovering from a drug addiction and alcoholism, and my father is a workaholic. Now I live with my grandparents. I pray to God every night and thank Him for my life, health, and wonderful family. I am so lucky to have my two incredible grandparents to take care of me. I believe that God gives you strength when you need it, and He would never give you something you could not handle. He is always forgiving and helps me through the tough times. I believe that there is a God, and He is looking out for each and every one of us. If you search really hard, you can feel the love of God through others. God is incredible and will never give up on you. All you have to do to find Him is reach out.

CLAIRESSE, 15

. . . CONSIDER GOD'S WONDERS . . .

Why do I believe in God? The question should be, Why
wouldn't you? There is one verse in the Bible that I have
loved since I was a little kid. It is Job 37:14, "'Listen to this,
Job; stop and consider God's wonders.'" This is simply
why I believe. You look at how things work, and you just
can't say there is no God.

ELI, 14

. . . WE HAVE TO MAKE OUR FAITH OUR VERY OWN . . .

As long as I can remember, I have gone to church with my family on a regular basis, and had a strong faith and commitment to the Lord. I was always brought up with good values and morals. I also had wonderful grandparents and great-grandparents with strong Christian values who set good examples for me, and I admire them. But as most teens know, we have to make our faith our very own and not something we inherit from our parents. I had to make the decision for myself whether I wanted to accept God as my Lord and Savior. Two summers ago, I went to a Christian youth camp. I wasn't expecting anything to happen that didn't usually happen every Sunday when I went to church. I was very wrong, and it was then that I owned my faith and made the decision that I wanted God in my life—not just because I was expected to go to church every Sunday, but because I wanted Him to be a part of my everyday life. I met other teens and realized that it wasn't just me who had to face temptations and hardships, and that I wasn't alone.

I also discovered that when things like that do come up

and someone isn't there to help me, I can just ask God, and He will give me the strength to face anything. No matter what, God accepts me for who I am and won't turn His back on me like a friend or boyfriend might. I have experienced miracles within my own family and have been blessed in feeling the comforting peace that God gives me when it seems no one else can. I have learned to trust the Lord with my future and live for Him daily. Whenever I have a problem, God is the first One I turn to. Under any circumstance, He is always there. He has filled my heart with joy.

JAIME, 15

I FEEL BLESSED . . .

I believe in God because He is always there whenever I have a problem. I know He will always be there guiding me toward the right path. I know that He hears me because when I am in doubt about something, I pray, and then I better understand what I should do. I feel blessed because God has been around me ever since I was born. My parents have always taught me to love God, and trust and respect Him by their example. I have learned, by trusting God, He will show me what to do and help me on my journey through life, every little step of the way.

JAKE, 15

ONCE I DISCOVERED GOD, I LEARNED . . .

I believe in God because He helped me to find myself. There was a point in my life when I had forgotten who I was. Everything around me was different. Kids at school were talking about me, and I started to believe everything that they were saying. It came to the point where I had to step out of my life, look at it, and change what was bad because when I looked at myself, I didn't like what I saw. My personality had become gray and colorless. My heart and my feelings were black and scarred. I was hurt and acting like someone I was not. I knew that I had to find something to grasp, to keep me strong and help me to find the real me. Finally, I found that something. It was a beautiful thing full of colors and everything good. For me, it was God. Once I discovered God, I learned that every time I have a problem or feel like I can't take it anymore, God will be there. He helped make me strong. I was able to look at my life again and see everything in a different light. My attitude toward life and my friends was full of joy and happiness. The scars on my heart were still there, but for every scar, I was ten times smarter. God taught me that I can take my life and learn from everything. Slowly, He healed my heart. God turned my life around, and that is why I believe. If you are like I was, I hope that you can find God, too.

KEISHA, 14

"T" TALK

A t the end of each chapter, you will find a "T" Talk from me, Mrs. T. I have chosen to use the "T" Talks to provide you with stories, spiritual insight, ideas, and guidance. If you find something of value, then I would ask you to embrace it. Take to heart that which is applicable to your life, and let it encourage and guide you as you grow in your faith.

Mrs. T

Chapter Two

Am I the Only One Who Only One Who Doubts God?

IF YOU FEED FAITH,

DOUBT STARVES . . .

If you have ever questioned the reality or presence of God, then the teen excerpts in this chapter may help you realize that you are not alone. However, I ask that you keep your heart open to the rest of the book because I believe you will find a hope that is so often born in faith. If you identify with a passage written in this chapter, please keep reading because, as the saying goes, "If you feed faith, doubt starves." At the same time, if you don't identify with this chapter because you have never doubted God, then I encourage you to take these questions and doubts to heart, as they will help you to be more understanding of others while you grow in your faith.

Mrs. T

WHERE WAS GOD WHEN I GOT DISSED?

I'm having a really tough time in my life. Sometimes, I feel lost and alone, and I can't find God. In one of those moments, I wrote this poem:

Where was God when I started to cry?

Where was God when I wanted to die?

Where was God when I felt left out?

Where was God when I screamed out?

Where was God when they judged me?

Where was God when no one would love me?

Where was God when I left my dad?

Where was God when I felt sad?

Where was God when I felt angry, violent,
   and depressed?

Where was God when they made fun of the way I dress?
Where was God when she broke up with me?
Where was God? He said He would always
   love me.
Where was God when I got pissed?
Where was God when I got dissed?
Where was God when my hopes died?

The more I bend, the harder they try.
Where was God when they put me down?
Where was God when they made me frown?
Where was God when I hated myself?
Where are you God? I need your help!

THOMAS, 14

I DO ENVY PEOPLE WHO BELIEVE IN GOD WITH NO DOUBTS . . .

Have you ever wondered if God is there? I do it all the time. I do not know if He really exists. Look at all the wars, hunger, and people who die unnecessarily. I know a lot of people ask these questions and doubt God. I do envy people who believe in God with no doubts or thought about it. I don't know if I could do it. Maybe the path to a perfect relationship or friendship with God is to have some doubts, just as we all usually doubt our friends about things they do, but we still trust them. The thing is, to do this, you have to have great faith, and that takes time. Maybe after some time and many trials and tribulations, I can believe that strongly. I am not saying that when I turn thirty, I will have a great revelation. It will take some time, but I hope one day I will become a Christian with strong convictions.

CORBIN, 17

. . . I WISH THAT GOD WOULD SHOW ME A SIGN . . .

Wherever I go, I hear about God. God this and God that. People say they believe in God because something happens to them or there was a sign. Sometimes, I wish that God would show me a sign so that I could believe. I've tried to believe, but as I've gotten older, things have happened to me that cause me to still question if God is real. Also, I met some friends who have even worse problems than I have, so I ask, if there is a God, why would He let this happen to me and them? The more I think about it, the more I wonder. Why would God let people suffer so badly if He is so great? How do we know somebody didn't just make Him up? I hope someone didn't, though, because I really would like to believe.

RONALD, 15

YET, I DOUBT HIM . . .

Even though I am very blessed, I can't seem to find God in my life. Perhaps I am not searching for Him hard enough, or I am waiting for Him to come to me. I do not know. I have so much going on in my life. I don't feel like I can let anyone else in, even my Protector and Provider. I know the Lord is good to me, and I know He has given me incredible gifts. Yet, I doubt Him. I feel He will not be there to lead me to heaven. I fear He won't accept me. What if He doesn't understand me?

God, to me, is like a fact. Like, I know nature exists, and it contains great beauty and splendor, but I don't care. I know God is there, and He is doing so much for me, but I cannot directly see that. Therefore, it doesn't matter. It is a harsh realization that I feel no connection with my God, but I don't know what to do. It is really a sad situation. I feel like I have plenty of time to find Him, and that He will always wait for me.

However, even worse, I myself am waiting for something. I am waiting for that great lightning bolt or the booming voice from the sky. Still, I think the chances of such things happening are very slim. So what am I doing, really? I am fooling myself. I am buying myself time and using my confusion as an excuse for my lacking efforts. I know these things. But I don't feel any impetus causing me to get on the road to change. I have seen God. I find Him every day. He is in my parents, who sacrifice everything for my sister and me. He is in my dearest friends, who help me to see things differently and bring so much happiness to me. Most importantly, I find Him in the strangers, in the people who offer smiles for no reason and tell me to have a good day and really mean it. God is there. In fact, He is so close I could touch Him. However, these encounters with God are not enough. I cannot get true satisfaction from God's presence in others until I find Him in myself.

JANNESSA, 18

WHY DOES HE LET ALL THE GOOD KIDS DIE?

The concept of God confuses me. I just don't see how it is possible for a guy to make all of us little people. I have all of these questions: If there is a God, then who made Him? How can He know everything about everyone? How can He control every event that happens? Why does He let all the good kids die? But, on the other hand, how would all of us be here if not for God? I mean, everything has its maker. For instance, buildings don't just pop up without anyone making them, so isn't it the same with all of creation? Like our bodies—they're just perfect. We have everything we need, like eyes, ears, a nose, and all of our organs. It's like someone designed us. So when I think that way, I think there must be a God. I still feel confused, though.

BILLY, 14

. . . IT IS VERY HARD FOR SOME PEOPLE TO BELIEVE IN SOMETHING THEY CANNOT SEE AND TOUCH . . .

Today, in a world of sin and betrayal, it is very hard for some people to believe in something they cannot see and touch. I am one of those people. I find it hard to believe in something if I have never totally witnessed it. Primarily, I think it is hard to find an honest and trustworthy person, let alone God. Finding an honest person today is like finding a diamond in the rough. Finding God, I think, is even more difficult. I have never seen or touched Him, and there is no scientific proof that He even exists. Although there are times when I feel I need Him, I am scared to pray to Him because I don't really have faith. I feel like a hypocrite if I pray and ask for His help. For me, faith in God is a very confusing thing. I have yet to really begin my religious journey, and I am truthfully not in any hurry. However, I know there will be a time in my life that I will have to turn to God. I hope at that time that God will lead me through my confusion.

SARAH, 17

. . . DOES HE THINK I THINK HE'S THERE?

When I was asked to write for this book, this poem flowed right from my heart to the paper. These are questions that I ask every day:

Is He really there?

Does He really hear my prayer?

Does He ever sit and stare?

Does He know my every thought?

Does He know when I've been caught?

Does He hear when I'm in doubt?

Does He know when I shout?

Does He know when I'm hurt?

Does He know when I flirt?

Does He think I think He's there?

Does He really even care?

Does He ever really know?

How can He ever show?

Can He help me when I'm down?

Can He save me when I frown?

Does He really have the power
   to sit and make the whole world cower?

Is He able to make me share
   all the things I wouldn't dare?

Does He know when I am wrong?

Does He know when I can't be strong?

Does He ever stand right by
   when I sit alone and cry?

Is He really there for me
   when no one else is there to see?

Should I ever really believe
   in something that I must conceive?

Is there some way to show me how
   He's really there, here and now?

DEENA, 16

. . . I AM CONFUSED AND DOUBTFUL . . .

Like Thomas in the biblical book of John, I am questioning my faith. I have gone through nine years of a private religious school, and during this time I have been told that God exists and that I do believe in Him. In all those years, I have never been asked if I actually do believe in God. Like Thomas, I would like to be shown that Jesus and God are real. Now that I have been asked, for the first time, what I believe in, I am confused and doubtful, and like many others I have questions that need to be answered. Will Jesus let me feel the wound in His side or give me another sign? Or will I have to discover faith on my own?

MANDIE, 16

MY EMPTINESS HAS BECOME A PUDDLE OF TEARS . . .

Sometimes I would question God and ask him why he was letting my life play out to be like it is. I would ask Him why my dad wasn't around, why he didn't pay child support, and why he would only call once a year or maybe twice if I was lucky. I had so many questions. Was God listening? After age eleven, it didn't mean too much to me when my dad would send an "I love you" card in the mail because he was never there. I had to mature so much faster than everyone else because of this. And I never really knew what happened to my dad. I was told that I was "too young to understand." But guess what? I grew up. No mom *and* dad for me, just mom. That's when it finally hit me that my dad was never coming home and that this life I was living wasn't just a dream. Memories started to gather into a blur. My dad's voice was just a faint sound of disappointment. I fear now that my dad is just a stranger in the picture lying in my closet. I never see him. He rarely calls. No birthday gifts even. Instead, he sends me IOUs. My emptiness has become a puddle of tears, and I am thankful that I have other family to keep me from drowning in it. My dad's being there when I was really little was just something I took for granted. Sometimes I want to be three years old again, so he can throw me up in the skylight just once more. But then I realize that our past is vanishing. My dad doesn't honestly even know me; he is not a part of my life anymore. In my confusion, I pray. "God, where are You? Give me an answer to why this is my life. Help me resist wanting to have a perfect life. Why can't my dad be the one to tuck me in at night or take me to a father/daughter dance? Why can't I be someone who can call someone their father and actually be proud of it?" Instead, I have an empty place in my heart, just waiting for my dad's company. I have a challenge ahead of me to make sure that I don't follow in his footsteps and turn out like him. I must struggle to get over all this and overcome. So, I pray to God. And even as I wait for an answer, in all of my uncertainty, I know God has been there and has helped me through my life.

ALIX, 14

. . . MOST OF THE SUMMER
I SPENT DOUBTING . . .

I lost my best friend to leukemia this summer. His name was Justin. He taught me many things while he was here on Earth, but the main gift Justin gave me was to follow the Lord, who is guidance, and all will be okay. To be honest, most of the summer I spent doubting God, being afraid and mad at Him because I knew He would be taking my closest friend away from me. But on the night Justin died, I was driving home with my family, and I saw this giant orange harvest moon. Mind you, it was the beginning of July! For some strange reason, I felt as if this moon was God talking to me, telling me not to doubt Him, but to believe that Justin is in a better place, no matter how hard it was to see him go. My favorite quote from the Bible is when Jesus spoke to the people and said, "I am the light of the world. Whoever follows Me will never walk in darkness, but will have the light of life.' (John 8:12)" That night in July, I saw the light of Jesus. His light led me from doubting God to knowing that I do not have to see to believe.

CIARRA, 14

. . . I LOST FAITH IN GOD . . .

Last year, confusion and sadness were daily issues in my life. My relationship with my best friend had fallen apart, and I honestly thought my world was over. Because of my lost friendship, I lost faith in God. I refused to go to church, and I couldn't stand it when people prayed in front of me. But then, over the summer, I met some new people, and my faith was renewed. I found out that my friendships with other people have a lot to do with my friendship with God. It wasn't God's fault that I had a falling-out with a friend. Maybe if I had listened to God, I would have recovered more quickly. He had better things waiting for me. I just didn't know it.

HEIDI, 14

... I DOUBTED THERE WAS SUCH A THING AS GOD ...

I believe in God, but I used to get confused. Sometimes, I thought, *God is up in heaven just hanging out.* And, sometimes, I thought, *There is no such thing as God.* I began thinking that after my brother died about seven years ago. He had some kind of rare cancer. I was only about six or seven, but I doubted there was such a thing as God. About two years after that, my mom went to jail. I was depressed a lot. I used to think, *If there was a God, He wouldn't let this all happen.* But I guess now I believe in God because I really don't have such a bad life. I mean, aside from all the usual bad stuff, my life is not all that bad. And I have come to see that what happens, happens. My mom made choices that landed her in jail. That's just life. If none of the bad stuff would have happened to me, I wouldn't be who I am today. So I guess, in a way, I am glad God didn't change anything. I believe in God again, and I like who I am. Me.

RESHAUD, 14

... HE WOULD BE LEFT A QUADRIPLEGIC ...

When I was around the age of six, my father was diagnosed with a brain tumor. This was a lot to handle at my young age. After the surgeons operated on the brain tumor, I did not understand what had happened; I just knew that this was not the father I remembered. My father's tumor was the size of a lemon and attached to the motor strip, a part of your brain that controls movement. The surgeons who operated on my dad were afraid that if they removed the entire tumor, he would be left a quadriplegic, paralyzed from the neck down. Days after the operation, I was finally allowed to visit my father. He sat propped up in bed, disoriented, and wondering who I was. No moment has ever in my life left me feeling so alone. With time, my father gradually became better, though he had to relearn almost every aspect of human life. Eventually, life finally began returning to the normalcy I so deeply yearned for. This may sound like things turned out fine, but about a year and a half later, my father's tumor began growing back, and he had to go in for chemotherapy. This was very scary to me when I was younger because he lost his hair and became sick. I was especially sad if I got sick because then I couldn't be with my father as it would put him at risk. For the next six or seven years, my father battled his tumor. When I became older, I started to ask myself why this was happening, and why it was *my* father and *my* family. I started to wonder what sort of God would let this happen to my dad and put my family in this vulnerable position. I was confused and began to lose my faith. Eventually, though, after talking to my priest and gaining his insight, I came to believe that perhaps God was testing my faith through everything that had happened. Maybe there was a reason for it all, even if I couldn't understand that reason. All of a sudden, it felt like a giant burden had been lifted off my shoulders, and my faith was restored.

STANLEY, 14

I AM CONFUSED ABOUT GOD . . .

I have been confused many times throughout my life. I entered ninth grade thinking it was going to be as easy as seventh and eighth grade. In the seventh and eighth grade, your teachers baby you more, but when I got into ninth grade I felt like I was on my own. There are so many more responsibilities. I had never spent an entire weekend just doing homework until ninth grade. My friendships also changed. I realized that the friends I grew up with weren't such good friends to me anymore, but I also made a lot of new friends. There have been weeks when my life is so hectic that I wonder if there is a God. There have been times that I pray for things to get better, yet they don't. Sometimes I feel like I should just run away, but then I realize how many people I would miss and who would miss me. God is so confusing! I don't go to church as much as I should, so I feel like I should be punished, or I think that God should make my week bad or something. Why didn't I feel this way when I was younger? I hated going to church, but now it is something I like to do. See how confused I am? I am confused about God, yet I want to go to church. I am confused about life right now. I don't even know how to fix it or where to begin to fix my problems. I pray that things will just get better, and sometimes they do. I just remember, or try to remember, that God never gives us more than we can handle.

GINA, 14

. . . IF THERE WAS NO GOD, THEN WHAT WAS . . .

When I was in the eighth grade, I began to doubt God. I was questioning everything I had always been taught, like that there was a God and that this God was all-loving and -forgiving. I was asking questions, and I wasn't getting any answers. Also, at the time, my parents were fighting a lot, and my older brother had just left for college, so I was feeling really alone. I prayed to God and asked Him to help my parents stop fighting and to give me all of the answers I needed. It didn't seem like God was even there. It just seemed like I was talking to nobody. None of my prayers were being answered, and my parents were getting worse. I was scared because if there was no God, then what was out there? Who was protecting us?

I started to not sleep. I just kept thinking about there not being a God, and I was always freaking myself out. I would stay up as late as I could because I didn't want to think about it, and if I went to bed, it would consume my thoughts.

My mom finally asked me what was wrong, and I told her that I doubted there was a God because of all the stuff that our family was going through. I told her how I prayed for help, and God never answered me. I told her about how I couldn't sleep at night because of it. So my mom started reading me this book about angels. It was filled with stories about people and how their guardian angel helped save their lives. She read to me until I fell asleep every night. By the time we finished the book, our family problems were starting to improve, I was getting my answers, and I could finally sleep at night. I felt like I had betrayed God by doubting His existence, but I remembered what I had been taught. God is all-loving and -forgiving—and I have never doubted Him again.

TOBYN, 17

"T" TALK

There have been various times in my life when I have doubted God. I think that we all probably have. Perhaps you currently question the presence or reality of God. Maybe you believe in God but have experienced a situation in your life that caused you to mistrust God or your faith. I remember a time when I doubted the most. My memory takes me back to my freshman year of college when my mom called to tell me that my friend, Dana, had been killed in a car accident. I was overwhelmingly saddened over the loss of my friend, but even more than that, I was angry at God for the injustice of it all. After everything that Dana had been through, I didn't understand why a loving God would let this tragedy occur. You see, just a few years before, when Dana was sixteen and living in northern California with her dad, she was involved in her first car accident.

Dana's sunroof was open in her sporty little car as she slowed to a stop on the frontage road that met with her long driveway. As she waited to turn, the driver of a semitruck came barreling along the road behind her. By the time he realized that her car was stopped, it was too late. Upon collision, the impact was so extreme that Dana was ejected through the sunroof and thrown far into a field off the road. She landed with such force that, although there appeared to be no external injuries, she suffered from extensive internal trauma. Dana was in a coma for over six weeks, during which time her parents feared that she would die. As they prayed for her recovery, Dana fought deep inside her damaged body to live. Amazingly, she did.

The severity of Dana's brain injuries meant she had to learn the most basic tasks all over again. With determination, she started to talk, walk, and regain control of her arms and hands. It was as if she was a mere toddler, taking baby steps. Each accomplishment was a praise to God. Several months after the accident, Dana moved in with her mom and stepdad. Although she continued to struggle with her speech and short-term memory, Dana finally felt that she had her life back. In fact, her best friend later told me that she thought Dana was perhaps more at peace than she had ever been.

Following her accident, Dana shared a wonderful relationship with her mom and stepdad. They were extremely close and came to appreciate each other in a way they hadn't before. Dana began going to church with her mom and accepted God into her life. She had graduated from high school and fell in love. Life looked bright! And now this. How could it happen to one person twice? I didn't understand. Why did she fight so hard to live, when she was going to die just a few short years later? Why would God take her, when He had given her such a wonderful second chance at life?

None of it made sense to me. It occurred to me at the time that if God would let something like this happen, then I didn't know if I wanted to believe in Him. I questioned how He could even be real, because in my mind a real and loving God would not have caused her parents, fiancé, and friends this much pain. He would not give them the hope of her life, only to snatch it away. For that matter, He wouldn't have given Dana the faith in a new start merely to deprive her of it before it even began. How could He?

Dana's mom was the one to answer that question for me. She explained that instead of feeling cheated, she felt blessed by God with the gift of three more years. Had Dana died after her first accident, they would not have had such quality time together these last few years. They had learned and loved so much. It was a time to treasure and be grateful for, she told me. I realized then that it was all about perspective. If Dana's mom could praise God during this time of tragedy, then why couldn't I? When I started to look at it from her point of view, I grew spiritually and personally. I came to realize that had I not doubted God, I would not have grown. The best part of my newfound insight, though, was that God understood my lack of faith.

Furthermore, I don't believe that doubting God hurts His feelings. Instead, I trust that it gives Him an opportunity to teach and love us. I understand how easy it is to jump into anger and frustration, put up a wall, and turn your back on God. The sad part is that this doesn't benefit us in any way. Doubting God's presence and power is natural, but it is also lonely. When we allow ourselves to believe that God sees a bigger picture than we do, that His vision is incomprehensible to us, we might find acceptance in our doubt. We likely will not understand why we must experience sadness and loss, trial or tragedy, but we can find peace in our acceptance that God knows.

A friend of mine once used the analogy of a hole in a fence to help answer the questions of life situations that don't seem to make sense. She said that as people living in God's creation, it is like we are standing behind a fence. On the other side of the fence, a parade is passing by. Unfortunately, the fence is tall, and we cannot see over it to glimpse a view of the parade. So we look through a little knothole that is present in a slat of the fence. We are able to see bits and pieces of the parade, but because our view is limited, we cannot conceive the entirety of the experience. This causes us to wonder why certain entries don't seem to match the theme or why a particular float is decorated in such a way. It is frustrating and confusing from our point of view. The colors don't flow. The bands are disconnected. We only see small portions of the floats, so it is difficult to tell what they represent. And, most discouragingly, we don't know where the route leads. Yet, from God's viewpoint, the parade is marvelous. He can see the complete procession, and therefore He fully understands the journey.

I often think of this comparison when I question the purpose or outcome of certain situations in my life. Occasionally, I get frustrated when a person dies or experiences a hardship, and I hear someone else say, "Everything happens for a reason." For those of us who have felt the pain of losing a loved one or experiencing an injustice like hunger, neglect, or abuse, there doesn't seem to be any "reason" on this Earth that is good enough. I have frequently felt that such a statement is extremely superficial. And yet, in a sense, this is where

I now find hope. If we do not have the answers, then God does. Someday, we will understand. However, in our present lack of understanding, we can grow, learn, and accept God's love and comfort for us.

Keep in mind, faith is a journey. If you don't ask questions, then how can you learn and grow? You have to start somewhere. For you, like some of the teens who wrote for this chapter, that place might be outright disbelief. If so, that is okay. Yet I would hope that you will read this book with an open heart. For if you are open, then perhaps there will be something written on these pages that you can identify with. Maybe a teen will share an experience that is similar to something you have faced. Hopefully, through this book you will discover some answers to questions that have always confused you and create in you a desire to know more about God.

Also, know that if you do doubt God, your skepticism may have originated from an issue related to a specific religion. I pray that through this book you will find that turning to God does not have to be about religion; more important, it is about a relationship. I have spoken with many teens, as well as adults, who have been turned off by religion. Perhaps they have observed hypocrisy within a particular church, or maybe they don't agree with certain rituals. As such, religion can occasionally be the basis for disbelief. Please don't assume that I am saying religion is wrong, because I am not. Actually, religion can give us a foundation, structure, and a community with which to enjoy fellowship. But religion without relationship can be meaningless. God calls you into a relationship with Him. When Jesus died and was resurrected, He sent the Holy Spirit so that you could have God with you always, so that you could know God, feel Him, and have a relationship with Him. Qualities of a healthy relationship include conversation, understanding, loyalty, and love. The Bible promises that God is committed to this type of relationship and desires it with you.

On the other hand, if you have already accepted the Lord into your life, then you know how wonderful and fulfilling a relationship with Him can be. Frequently, people who consider themselves believers feel guilty if or when they doubt God. If you have ever felt this way, please know that God understands it when we question Him. He doesn't condemn us for our doubt. A Christian leader once told me that he believed that God actually liked us to doubt. He said, "Without doubt, we sometimes get stagnant in our relationship with God. Yet when we ask questions of God, we become energized to find the answers." And even if you don't find the answers that you may be looking for, as many teens shared in this chapter, God will still be waiting for you when you are ready to turn to Him. He is also prepared to guide you from your disbelief and help you rediscover your faith.

Despite your current spiritual beliefs, there is a reason that we doubt. Doubt causes us to question. As we question, we discover; as we discover, we grow. It is likely that our life journeys are going to take us down different roads. But if we welcome growth upon our path through life, it will enrich our hearts and fill us with hope. As you read through the pages of this book, I pray that you open the door to your heart and allow your faith to grow.

Mrs. T

Chapter Three

GOD, GRANT ME COURAGE

. . . THE LORD PROVIDES US WITH COURAGE . . .

We all encounter situations in our lives in which we experience a need for courage. Our reasons may be extremely simple or quite complex. Some of the teens who wrote for this chapter share serious problems that led to their prayer for courage. Others express a need for boldness that stems merely from ordinary teen angst. Despite the reasons, I hope that the passages you are about to read will lead you to think about the many ways the Lord provides us with courage and strength. I also pray that if you read a passage that you have difficulty identifying with because of a sensitive topic such as suicide or addiction, you will use that excerpt to help you understand what a fellow student or a close friend may be experiencing. Let these stories give you insight and understanding. Perhaps they may even give you the courage to reach out and help someone in need.

Mrs. T

I WORRIED ABOUT
EVERY POSSIBLE THING THAT
COULD GO WRONG . . .

I used to think courage was a gift given only to a select few; a person either had it or she didn't. I think many people, especially teens, feel the same way. The last place most people would look for courage would be in God, but I found courage, as well as strength, in God. When I was young, I truly believed I was fearless; I could remember not being afraid of anything. I wasn't scared to try new things, to go against the norm, or to be the person I was inside.

I am not sure exactly when that all changed, but I think it was around the time I entered high school. For the first time in my life, I was nervous on the first day of school. I wasn't a nervous type of person; in fact, I rarely got nervous, but that day I was so nervous I almost felt sick. It seemed odd to me to get so worked up about something as silly as school, but I couldn't help myself. I worried about every possible thing that could go wrong; at the time, I didn't think I had ever been so scared in my life. On the way to school that morning, I looked to God. I felt that

He was the only one who could make me feel any better. I didn't ask God to take away my nervousness or to make everything go perfectly on my first day of high school. I simply asked Him to be with me because I felt that I needed Him. I walked into school that morning, and I felt that God was with me. He filled me with courage. My nervousness didn't disappear, but it was eased, and that was all I needed.

HOLLI, 18

. . . HE WOULD JUST BEAT HER . . .

When I was a young boy and my parents were still together, my father would verbally and mentally abuse my mother. My dad would usually get drunk and then either tear my mom apart verbally nonstop until she was in tears, which could take multiple hours depending on how mad he was, or he would just beat her. Thank God my mom finally got out and got a divorce before anything worse happened. Even though my parents were divorced, my sister and I still had to go see him. We had to spend every other weekend with my dad. I dreaded those weekends because he would still come home, get drunk, and then start to verbally abuse me and my brother. He did this so often that we eventually started to believe what he was telling us. We didn't have any confidence or a feeling of self-worth since every time we saw him, he would tell us that we weren't worth two cents, or that we were a mistake. Those were just a few of the nicer things he would tell us. One night, my dad and my brother had a really big fight. My dad was still upset with him the next day. He told my brother that if he told my mom anything about their fight, the police would find his body at the bottom of the local river. That was the last time we ever saw my dad. You see, my brother didn't listen to our dad's threat; he found the courage to speak up. Thankfully, through the grace of God and lots of prayers, my whole family was able to leave my father's house for good without getting too hurt. If God wasn't present in my mom's life, she never would have had the courage to leave my dad. Her example helped us to have the courage to handle our ordeal because we knew that God would lead us in the right direction to get us far away from my father. Without God present in all our lives, my mom would probably be dead, and my brother and I would be extremely psychologically messed up. With God, everything is possible, no matter how big or small the problem. He will always be there for you. All you have to do is put your faith in Him and know everything will work out for the best, just like it did in my life.

KENDRICK, 17

. . . EVEN IN MY LONELIEST HOUR, I HAVE NEVER FELT ALONE . . .

Mark Twain once said, "Be good, and you will be lonely." Now what he didn't say is that being lonely is not the same as being alone. You see, throughout my life, I have always tried to be honest and do the right thing, even if it wasn't the most popular choice. Hence, some of these choices have thrown me into a state of loneliness. However, even in my loneliest hour, I have never felt alone. There has always been a light in the darkness, a voice in the silence, an existence in the void. God has always been my sentinel, watching over and protecting me when I truly needed a guardian. God has also given me the courage and the strength to pull myself out of these states of loneliness. Unlike Icarus, from Greek mythology, who had no one to catch him when he fell from the heavens, I feel that God is always by my side, ready to fix my wings and allow me to fly again.

JAMES, 17

I HAD NEVER THOUGHT SERIOUSLY ABOUT SUICIDE BEFORE . . .

About a year ago my life couldn't get any worse. My best friend had died, my mother was abusive, my father absent, and my sister on a downward spiral using drugs. I felt like nothing could make my life better. I felt worthless. That night I started thinking that if my life was eventually going to end anyway, I might as well do it myself now so that I wouldn't have to suffer anymore. Though I had never thought seriously about suicide before, I found myself in my room with two bottles of pain medication. I figured it wouldn't hurt if I overdosed on pills. So I turned on my music, getting ready for my death. I sat down on my bed with the pills in hand as a song started to play. It was one of my favorite songs. It was from a CD my youth pastor made for me and the lyrics went something like this: "You're not alone, you're not alone. He'll never leave you. . . . " And it made me do sorta like a double take on my life. It reopened my eyes to who I was. All the bad things that had happened in my life had helped me to actually become a strong person, not one who would take the easy way out. What I realized was that even though I had no comfort at home and no one really understood what I was going through, God understood and He could comfort me. You might think it was a coincidence that song came on. I don't. I know that God works in mysterious ways. God gave me courage to live instead of die. I took the courage He gave me and started living my life according to His plan.

KANDACE, 16

AUTHOR'S NOTE: Kandace suggests that when everything in her life was going wrong, she thought of ending her life. Please recognize that instead of turning to suicide, Kandace turned to God. Taking one's life is not the answer and definitely not God's desire for you. If you have ever contemplated suicide, please seek comfort and courage from God, and find the strength in Him to talk to someone about what you are feeling or to call the National Suicide Hotline at 1-800-SUICIDE (1-800-784-2433). Also, please take time right now to refer to the "T" Talk at the end of this chapter for reassurance and guidance.

. . . I THOUGHT FITTING IN WOULD BE THE MOST IMPORTANT THING IN MY LIFE . . .

When I was younger, the realization that I was fat came from other people's hurtful words and mean comments. I would always try to hide from people and their words. I would cry so much, and my tears would sting my cheeks with shame for myself and what I looked like. Because I thought fitting in would be the most important thing in my life, it just made me feel even more excluded. I kept to myself, and I avoided people. Yet, they came and found me, just to put me down and make fun of the way I looked. I was always in tears, but no one saw them. No one saw the pain I was really feeling because I hid behind a plastic smile and fake laugh. I was lost and confused, and I didn't know where to go. Whenever I went out to recess, they would make a game out of hurting my feelings or making me cry. I was always in tears, and my friends weren't even there when I needed them the most. They would say that they felt sorry for me but were too afraid it would hurt their own image if they stuck up for me. I had no one, and

I was too alone to be human. I felt one-of-a-kind and hated it. Then I went to a youth group, and my eyes were opened because I saw Christ. He opened not just my eyes but also my heart. He gave me the courage to love myself for who I was and not what I looked like. I asked Him to lift my problems off my shoulders. He helped me through everything. He showed me that it is great to be one-of-a-kind and that is exactly what I am.

MADDISON, 13

WAS I REALLY BEING
LEFT ALONE?

Growing up, my life was okay. We had some tough times, but we always knew we would get through it as a family. I lived with my dad and my brother, and I always knew we would be all right. But when I was thirteen, our family started falling apart. I'm not sure how it all came about, but little things created heated arguments. My dad and older brother were constantly crashing into each other in an endless battle of who was right.

One night stands out the most to me because I discovered a faith that was stronger than the anger. My dad and brother were fighting (nothing new), but this time was far worse. I was brought into it. I felt harsh words lash out at me from my father with cold cruelness. At that point, I would have rather experienced physical pain than hear what he had just said to me. My dad, full of rage and fury, put on his jacket and took off. My brother, in the same state of mind, was packing his stuff, preparing to run away. I felt my world caving in around me. Was I really being left alone? I didn't want the fights, but I didn't want to be alone either. My brother left the room, and at that moment I felt completely hopeless. I hit the ground with angry tears streaming down my face and begged God to help me. I asked Him to give me the courage it would take to be the one to hold it together. I asked Him to give them both forgiveness for each other. In that instant, I felt about a thousand times lighter. Then my tears of frustration turned into those of determination. I got up and went out to find my dad. I made both my dad and brother come back to the house. I made them talk and, more important, I encouraged them to listen. For once in my life, they heard what I said.

Since then, things are getting better. A lot of time has passed, and it hardly ever gets that bad. I know God was with me that night, and I know He gave me the courage to reach the unreachable. I am not perfect when it comes to religion, but I am a believer. I know God was with me that night, and I know He will always be with me when I need Him. I have put my trust in God's hands. I know that with Him, I will be safe. It doesn't matter what this life brings; God will see me through it. I know great things are waiting for me. All I need to do is stay with God.

GABRIELLA, 15

SHE HAS HERSELF AND HER FAMILY FOOLED . . .

I'm worried about a friend of mine. Maybe you have a friend like this, too. I put my thoughts down in this poem:

I have this friend, we've been friends forever
But now our friendship doesn't seem to measure
She's lost so much weight in this past year
If she doesn't seek help, the end will be near
She has herself and her family fooled
Her obsession with being skinny has overruled
When I try to talk
She gets mad and walks
Although I know deep inside
She isn't mad, she is just trying to hide
She's quit the sports she's loved and been
    good at
Because now her body won't let her do that

I have thought and thought of what to do
My other friends feel it is their fault, too
My friends and I have done everything we
    possibly could
I hope she'll turn to God for courage, like
    she should
There is nothing left for me to do
But to know that God will help her through

NINA, 14

AUTHOR'S NOTE: Eating disorders are extremely dangerous and need to be taken seriously, as they can threaten one's health and life. If you currently are struggling with an eating disorder, please allow yourself to reach out for help. Talk to your parents, pastor, friends, or an adult whom you trust. You may also find it helpful to contact Eating Disorders Awareness and Prevention (EDAP), an eating-disorder information and referral hotline, at 1-800-931-2237.

I THANKED GOD FOR GIVING ME THIS PEACE IN MY HEART . . .

In the past six months, I have really gotten a lot of courage and strength from the Lord. I come from a very extensive Native-American family, and we all love each other with our hearts and souls. In the past six months, I have lost five loved ones, and this hurt me badly. It has been two months since the last death. I was close to all of them, especially my great-grandma. We shared the same soul. Although I felt angry that my loved ones were gone, I still found strength in the Lord.

About three days after my great-grandmother's death, I was feeling terrible, and I couldn't eat or get out of bed. I was dozing off to sleep when I heard three knocks on my bedroom window. I was frightened. I sat up on my bed and leaned against the wall. I saw a light. It wasn't very bright, but it was glowing. I heard two women laughing, and they sounded very happy. Not only did they sound happy, but they sounded like my beautiful great-grandma and my little auntie. She was my great-grandma's sister who passed away only three months before. I was no longer scared. I felt warm inside. I fell to sleep never saying a word or trying to speak to them, just listening to their sweet voices that used to whisper me to sleep. I woke up feeling peace, remembering the last time I saw my great-grandma. She told me, "Don't stay away too long," and I said, "You either." She said, "You better come visit me." I said, "You, too." And that's exactly what she did! I thanked God for giving me this peace in my heart, for I did not get to say good-bye before her death. Also, I thanked God for giving me the courage to accept my great-grandmother's death and go on with my life.

Luci, 14

. . . MY FATHER WAS DIAGNOSED WITH CANCER . . .

I recently got some bad news: my father was diagnosed with cancer. It didn't just end there, though. The cancer cells weren't contained and had spread to his lymph nodes. It was really hard on my whole family, but it would have been a hundred times harder if I didn't have faith. God gives me the courage and hope I need to make it through the day. With my dad always on my mind on top of school, friends, sports, and the million other things that I have going on, I don't know if I would be able to handle it all without my faith. All of my friends are keeping my dad in their prayers, along with me. Life is rough sometimes, and all we can do is have the courage to get through the difficult times. There is no one else who will be there the way God is 24/7. If there is anyone close to you who is sick, depressed, or lonely and needs you, let God be your refuge, your relief. No matter what the problem at hand, God is always there guiding you and helping you overcome your fears and hardships.

RENA, 15

. . . *I WOULD HEAR SOME OF THE CONVERSATIONS, AND I WOULD BE ASHAMED . . .*

Have you ever felt pressure to go along with a crowd, even when you didn't agree with them? Well, in the beginning of my junior varsity volleyball season, it happened to me. Some of my teammates had no respect for our coaches. They would talk behind the coaches' backs by calling them names and making rude comments. There were some girls who didn't want to be part of the drama, but they ended up getting involved. I think it was because the girls who started it were older and popular, and so it was tough for some not to get caught up in it. But there were others, like me, who chose to stay out of it completely, even though we felt the pressure. It was so hard because I would hear some of the conversations, and I would be ashamed of the girls who started it all because our coaches were great people. All of this drama ended up with some of the girls signing a petition to try to get the coaches removed. Through it all, I disagreed with what my teammates did. I really had to look to God for courage, because without it, I don't think I could have stayed on the team. Every night after practices or games, I would lie in bed and pray to God to give me and my coaches courage. On the team, I was often put in a bad position, but God always gave me the courage and strength to make the right choice and stand up for myself and my beliefs. My coaches were also put in awkward positions by these girls, but I know that God gave them the courage to get through it and still keep our team together as a family. Throughout the rest of the season, the drama kept building, but God helped me to ignore it and finish the season without too much worry. I feel a lot happier now that the season is over, and I believe my coaches probably do, too. For the rest of my life, because of this situation, I know that God will always be there to give me courage when I need it most. So if you have ever been in a pressured situation, look to God. I know that He will give you courage, too!

SHARAE, 14

I WAS SCARED
OUT OF MY MIND . . .

I was always confused when I was little. When I look back at how my life was, I don't think it was a very good one. Of course, I always had fun playing with my friend on the swings and stuff, but when it came to what went on at home, I didn't like it. My mom was always having new people over, people I had never even seen before. I thought they were going to be some new friends or something. I was a little confused about it, but I never asked because of what I can remember about my mom. She always seemed to be in a bad mood or not wanting to be around me at all.

One day, my mom did not come home at night. My dad got off work at 5:00. I was supposed to be picked up from school at 3:00. I had to sit at the school for two hours, and finally the cops had to come and pick me up. I was scared out of my mind. When I got home, my dad was just showing up. I was happy to be home, but scared and confused because I didn't know what was going on. That night, I found out that my mom was in jail for drugs. I was also confused about what drugs were. I learned that the people who always came to my house were people who were dealing drugs with my mom.

Eventually, my dad left my mom, and we moved and started over. I remember my new next-door neighbor came over to meet me, and I started talking to her. She had a lot of belief in God. I used to think that maybe there was no God because I didn't think He was ever there to help me. My new neighbor showed me that God was there. She said that maybe I experienced everything with my mom for some reason that I wouldn't understand until I was older. She also looked me in my eyes and said, "Nita, God does have faith in you to go to school, get good grades, and stand up for yourself. He will give you the courage you need." So I figured I would try to believe in myself. If God believes in me, maybe I could, too. And He did give me courage. Even with all my family problems, I do excellently in school, and I have a lot of new friends—mostly because I now have a really strong belief in God.

NITA, 14

AUTHOR'S NOTE: Sadly, some teens come from homes in which a parent is addicted to drugs or alcohol. If you or someone you know is living with an addict and needs help or support, I encourage you to contact your local chapter of Al-Anon, Alateen, or a similar program that provides support for families living with addicts. You can call 1-888-4-AL-ANON (1-888-425-2666) to find an organization near you.

"T" TALK

Joe was one of my best friends in high school. He was the type of guy whom everyone loved. He had a strong faith in the Lord, but at that time in his life, he lived for his friends. Although he was an outstanding athlete, he was able to supersede the typical high-school cliques. He was full of life and always ready for a fun time. One of the things I enjoyed most about Joe was the delight he took in luring someone into a good prank. Maybe I enjoyed it so much because he and I pulled many pranks on one another. One of Joe's favorite schemes, which he carried out with another close friend of ours, was to sneak into my locker, take the keys to my truck, and then move it to various places around our school. When I would go out to the parking lot after school, I'd never quite know where I'd find my truck. Once it was on the other side of the football field. Another time, it was behind the convenience store across the street. I never figured out how they pulled it off without getting into trouble, especially when they left it for me to find on our school's front lawn. The ultimate fun, however, was worth their efforts. It seems ironic now that while my truck was the source of so much amusement for us, Joe's truck carried him into the greatest tragedy of his life.

It was a typical Friday night in a small town. Joe and his friend, Ronnie, were on their way to a party. It was dark, and he and Ronnie were listening to the radio, cruising along. All of a sudden, Ronnie screamed, "Joe . . . STOP!" Within an instant, Joe felt a sickening thud and watched his right windshield shatter into pieces. Joe never saw the man who had wandered into the road, but the second he felt the impact, he knew that he had just hit a human being. Can you imagine what went through his mind? Joe told me later that everything inside him wanted to run. His first thoughts were, *Just keep driving*, as if ignoring this terrible calamity might make it go away. But he knew that his conscience would not allow that to happen. So Joe pulled to the side of the road. As he got out of his truck, he looked back to see a limp, mangled body. Ronnie raced to call for an ambulance, while Joe ran over to where the man lay lifeless in the middle of the road. He felt so helpless as he approached because as he encountered the man's crumpled body, he knew inside that the man was already dead.

While Joe waited for the police and ambulance to arrive, his own life flashed before his eyes. Questions filled his mind. How could this have happened? How could he have killed someone? How could his life change so fast? One moment, Joe was on his way to laugh, joke, and live it up with friends at a party, and in the next instant he was kneeling over a man, willing him to breathe. It didn't seem fair. He wasn't driving recklessly, drinking, or even speeding. The road was clear, and then out of nowhere there was this man.

As these thoughts swirled around in Joe's mind, he subtly began to feel a very small sense of peace. He couldn't explain this feeling except to say that it could only have come from God, for the circumstances that he had found himself in were too overwhelming to even comprehend. As statements were taken, Joe learned that the man he had hit was homeless and had been walking along the road with another man. The man told the police that he had told his friend not to walk in the road. But the victim had been drinking and had lost his sense of good judgment. He had no identification, family, or home. While Joe was taken to have his blood tested to confirm that he had not been drinking, the man was taken to the morgue. All the while, Joe's heart was pounding with the reality of the accident. Yet, he knew that he had to focus on the sense of peace he was feeling because, without it, Joe knew that fear would overwhelm him.

Mostly, Joe feared that all of his dreams and desires for the future would vanish as quickly as this horrifying accident that had just transpired. He feared he would lose control of his life and his destiny. You see, Joe had always wanted to be a cop. It had been his goal for as long as he could remember. Would he never realize this dream? Or worse, would he end up on the other side of it, behind bars? Joe also feared the reaction of his family and friends. What would they think, and what would they say? Throughout the days following the accident, Joe contemplated all of these things and knew he had an important decision to make. He could give up and hide behind his fears, or he could seek the courage he would need to face the repercussions of this tragic ordeal.

Joe chose to grasp on to that underlying peace that had been steadfast throughout his fear and confusion. Daily,

Joe put his situation in God's hands, and that sense of peace nurtured a feeling of courage that he knew he would not have experienced on his own. Joe knows that without God's touch, he could have withered away. But with God, he was able to hold his head up, face his fears, and grow emotionally, as well as spiritually.

I, on the other hand, struggled with my role as Joe's friend. How do you support someone who has experienced something so tragic? As a sixteen-year-old, I was scared. On the day following the accident, I picked up the phone to call Joe fifteen different times but hung up before I dialed because I was afraid that I would say the wrong thing. When I finally did make the call, I was relieved when Joe's mom told me that he wasn't up to talking. I comforted myself with, "At least you tried." I could have done so much more, but I just didn't have the courage. I remember praying for Joe, but not praying for myself to find the courage to be the friend that Joe needed me to be in his time of need.

I understand now that the courage we tend to lack as teens can be found in the strength and power of God. Had I asked God to give me the courage to comfort my friend, I believe I would have had the confidence to show up on his front doorstep, if only to say, "I'm here for you." But, I was afraid, so I made excuses. As teenagers, it is easy to make up a reason for not taking action by convincing ourselves that it is for the better. When really, we may just not have the courage it takes to do the right thing. I told myself that Joe needed his space, that he didn't want to see anyone and needed time with his family. It took me almost a week to work up the courage on my own to get over to Joe's house and be there for him as a friend. Yet, in the Bible, Jesus says, "Ask

and it shall be given unto you, seek and you shall find."
Courage is waiting in that scripture. As I look back, I wish
that I would have sought such strength from God.

If you have struggled with an experience in your life where
you have needed the courage to endure, look to God. When
someone dies, for example, it seems so senseless to us, so
unfair. We get lost in our grief, and that is a very lonely place
to be. Sometimes we even turn our backs on God. But turning toward God instead of away from Him can bring understanding, peace, and even hope to your heart.

Maybe your need for courage is more serious. Perhaps
you need it because you question the value of your own life.
If, like Kandace, you have ever considered suicide, please
know that taking your own life is not the answer to your
hopelessness. I have heard teens occasionally express that
they feel it takes courage to commit suicide. I disagree. I
believe that it takes courage to live. Think about this: If your
life is so bad that you consider suicide as your only option,
then it has to get better. And if it is going to get better, why
would you want to die?

I have spoken to numerous teens who have admitted to
thinking about suicide. So know that if you have ever considered it, you are not alone. Yet that doesn't mean that
attempting suicide, let alone completing it, is right. One of my
former students, Anthony, told me that when he gets in the
mind-set of having nothing left to live for, he turns it around
and considers that if, in fact, that is the case, then he has
nothing left to lose. This keeps him focused on living rather
than dying. Another student, Summer, once shared that she
saw her life as an endless book. Each page was a new day.
She said that if teens get to the point where they are consid-

ering suicide, then all they need to do is wait until the next day because it is a whole new page, and who knows what excitement or happiness could be waiting there. Just like a book, our life stories change. If we take it upon ourselves to end our lives, we miss out on the story in its entirety, and the story could have an incredibly happy ending.

In addition, when contemplating suicide, teens frequently neglect to think about the people they would hurt by their choice. They tend to disregard the consequences of fatal actions. Do you think that God, who loves you so much, who in essence created you and gave you life, would want you to take your life into your own hands? Have you ever asked yourself if suicide isn't, in reality, murder? Now, I'd be willing to bet that you would never think about killing another person, so why would you kill yourself? In God's eyes, perhaps it is the same. What do you think?

Regardless of your answer, know that God has a gift waiting for you. It is not wrapped in beautiful paper with a perfect bow. In fact, He has already opened it and placed it in a small room in your heart. It is courage, and it is waiting there to be discovered by you. When you do find it, if you keep your eyes focused on God as you approach, the courage He has placed in your heart will blossom into the strength that you need to see you through your most difficult trial or turbulent time. Like my friend Joe, if you put your life in God's hands daily, He will give you the courage you need to persevere.

Mrs. T

AUTHOR'S NOTE: If needed, please take time to turn to Appendix II at the end of the book for additional referral services for grief and loss, suicide, drug addiction, eating disorders, and more.

Chapter Four

YOU ARE MY STRENGTH!

... THE LORD WILL PROVIDE YOU WITH COURAGE AND STRENGTH ...

Some of the excerpts written in this chapter deal with very serious issues. Teens write of experiences such as drug use, abuse, and grief. Although I understand that these topics are quite extreme, I have chosen to include them in this chapter to demonstrate that even in the most desperate of situations, the Lord will provide you with courage and strength to endure such life experiences. I realize that you may read this chapter and think, Gosh, my life experience is mild compared to some of these people. Why would God take time for my little problems? Know that God does take time because He loves you. If you need the strength to deal with the pressures of achieving academically or meeting your parents' expectations, God will provide. Or perhaps you've prayed for the courage to reach out and make a new friend. God knows the importance of your prayer. You don't need to be dealing with a severe situation to call out to God for strength. On the other hand, if you do identify with some of the serious issues addressed in this chapter, feel free to turn to the "T" Talk at the end of the chapter for reassurance and advice. Also, pray for the courage to talk to a trusted adult. Regardless, please know that whatever your situation, mild or extreme, God will be there.

Mrs. T

I DON'T HAVE THE COURAGE OR THE STRENGTH IN ME TO STAND UP AND SAY NO . . .

I will be the first one to admit that I don't have a strong personality. Peer pressure is a hard thing for me to deal with because of that. I don't have the courage or the strength in me to stand up and say no. Sometimes I end up doing stupid things, and people get upset with me, but no matter what, God is always there. In some situations, I find it easy to just step back, reflect, weigh the consequences, and let God guide me to the right decision. I know that He can provide me with the strength to say no if I honestly don't want to regret a potential poor choice because of peer pressure. So when I don't have the strength to say no, I look to God and use His strength.

BRIANNA, 15

I RETURNED FROM MY VACATION UNCERTAIN OF WHERE WE WERE TO LIVE . . .

"You are a strong person" were the only comforting words I received from my father when he told me there had been a fire and we had lost everything. I had been camping with a friend during one of the hottest weeks of July 1999 when a fire spread across the six-family apartment building where I lived, leaving nothing to spare. I returned from my vacation uncertain of where we were to live and how we were going to survive. While finding a place to live and buying new belongings through donated money, I began to feel very frustrated with God. My head was filled with questions. *Why me? Why did my home have to burn down? Why did my parents have to be divorced? Why couldn't I have a normal life?* Eventually, I realized I had no right to be frustrated with God; in fact, I should be thankful that He had given me these experiences. God had allowed these things to happen to me not because He wanted to see me suffer, but because He knew I could handle them. I began to see that through my trials, God led me to become a stronger person.

RANDEE, 18

IN MY HEART, I KNEW WHAT I HAD TO DO . . .

My senior year of high school was definitely an experience . . . full of fun and friends, but also trials. When finals rolled around, my brain was not the only thing being tested; my heart and my conscience were as well. About a week before the scheduled final for one of my hardest classes, a rumor began circulating that three guys in my class were going to steal our teacher's final. Very quickly, the bidding began. It felt like the entire class was offering to pay the guys as long as they got a copy of the final ahead of time. Right away, I was posed with three different choices.

My first option was to take advantage of this amazing opportunity. I mean, it's not every day that a final is available ahead of time, and I had so many to study for. I was nervous about all of my upcoming finals; having this one taken care of would definitely lighten my study load. I would only have to come up with the proper sum of money, deliver it to those gutsy guys, and I'd have it made: one A+ in the bag, baby!

My second option was slightly different, but at least it would save me money. I could not participate in this very risky and very illegal endeavor. I'd just ignore what it felt like everyone was doing, study for the final, and most definitely sulk as I saw my classmates receive their A+s.

The last option was by far the most difficult. Up until this time, what I did affected no one. If I joined them, they'd be happy (at least about the extra money), and if I stood by and minded my own business, they wouldn't care. My problem was that little cricket sitting on my shoulder and screaming in my ear.

The voice of the cricket was, of course, God. In my heart, I knew what I had to do. I had to tell my teacher what was going on; he had to know the plot to steal the final. Doing this would surely provide me with a long list of brand-new enemies, all foaming at the mouth, ready to kill me for spoiling their A+s. The strength to go to my teacher, knowing full well how many people would hate me after I did, was not my own, but the Lord our Father's.

The afternoon I chose to divulge my information felt like an eternity. As I walked up the seemingly endless steps to my teacher's office, a voice in my head kept repeating to me: your rewards will not come in this life, but in heaven. That voice was the only thing that made me climb those steps. All the way up, there was a screaming match going on inside my head because there was also a voice crying out that I was flushing a perfectly good A+ down the toilet. Anyway, I made it up the steps and was somehow able to muster the courage to knock on my teacher's door and take a seat across from him at his desk. I told him the truth, the whole truth, and nothing but the truth (so helped by God, of course), and I actually survived. Many times, I told myself I could not face the situation, for it was just too difficult. But I did somehow, and the relief I felt after the fact was wonderful.

If left to my own human weakness, I have no doubt I would have given in, forked over the dough, and taken—

actually stolen—the A+. Instead, because of the strength from God, I know I did the right thing. I can look at myself in the mirror every morning with no shame and, actually, a bit of pride. I took the test, which my teacher undoubtedly made a great deal harder after I left his office, and got a B. My grades are very important to me, but I treasured this B, not for its value in my GPA, but for what it said. The strength I lacked to do the right thing was made up for by God, and that B will forever remind me!

MARIAH, 19

A SLEEPER WAVE CAME AND PULLED TWO OF MY BEST FRIENDS INTO THE FRIGID WATER . . .

In the eighth grade, my school basketball team entered a tournament on the northern California coast and stayed the weekend there. We, the team, had a great time hanging out with each other and enjoying the basketball tournament we played in, even though we were the worst team that attended. On our last day, minutes prior to our departure, we all decided to climb down to the tide pools to view the sea one last time. A sleeper wave came and pulled two of my best friends into the frigid water. The father of one of my other teammates, an ex-Navy Seal in his late fifties, dove in after them. He managed to save one friend but drowned in the process. One of my best friends and my teammate's dad died that day. This experience was so foreign to me and seemed unreal. I didn't know where to turn, so I turned to God. He gave me strength to be with friends and family in this time of need. He helped me to get over this tragic situation by helping me feel fortunate for what I have—great family and friends—and to be thankful for every day I live on this Earth. I was given the strength to continue living life, without forgetting this tragedy. I remember the heroics of my friend's dad as he put the lives of two boys before himself, and I will never forget him or my great friend who also drowned that day. God has given me the strength to remember them, yet to move on simultaneously. When I think back to the two people who died that day, I remember their character and the good times with them, and I am happy that I even knew them at all.

Rusty, 18

THAT'S WHEN I GOT INTO DRUGS . . .

In the beginning of the sixth grade, my parents were starting to have some big problems. Each time they fought, the yelling and fighting seemed to get worse. About the middle of that year, my parents got a divorce. That devastated me. I have always relied on my family. Now my family was all broken apart. My little brothers and sisters were too young to understand, my mom didn't seem to care, and my dad was moving to another state. My life was falling apart. I started hanging out with some older friends all the way through that year. I noticed they were into drugs, parties, girls, and alcohol, but I didn't do that stuff because my mom and I were very close, and I didn't want to do that to her.

Well, about the summer before my seventh-grade year, my mom started seeing this guy. He was nice, very religious, and treated my mom like gold. I was happy for her at first, but then she started to get serious with him. She started spending all of her time with him and not much time with me. That's when I got into drugs. I started to hang out with those friends a lot more. All we did was drink, do drugs, go to parties, sneak out, and get into trouble.

My mom noticed the change in me. I was never home, I would talk back, my grades slipped badly, I hated her boyfriend, and I never did what she asked. I know she suspected that I was using, but she had no proof. Still, I was excluding myself from my good friends, my family, and my real self. My mom got worried, and she and her boyfriend sat me down and talked to me. They asked me if I was using drugs and all that stuff. I denied it all. I just told them what they wanted to hear.

We all got up, but then my mom's boyfriend pulled me to the side and asked me if I knew God. I said, "Of course, I know God. I've gone to church, and I know He is there." He said, "No, do you actually know God?" I was like, "No, I don't know Him." He told me a lot about God that night. He told me that I needed to open my eyes and realize that there is something greater than me. Then he asked me how my life was going. I said, "Good, I guess," but I knew that inside my life was in pieces. And I know he saw right through me. He said, "God is there. He will listen, and He will answer. He will be your strength." He also said, "If you don't believe me, just try to discover God yourself, but mean it." He challenged me that night to read the book of John from the New Testament. I did, and just reading that one book changed a lot of my thinking. I realized that there is someone greater than me, who has a never ending love for me and gave His Son for me. I sat in my bed that night, and I wept while asking God to forgive me for all that I had done and all the people I had hurt. I asked Him to help me in my ways, give me the strength to resist my temptations, and be with me.

As I began to focus on my grades and the important things in my life, I became closer with God. It hasn't always been easy, but my life became so much better. It turned out that everything my mom's boyfriend (now my stepdad) said was right. God provided me with love, strength, and a better life. If it wasn't for Him, I might not even be here right now. So, I ask you to believe. Put your faith in God and rest. You will be saved in more than one way. People and friends come and go, but the Lord remains forever.

REEVE, 15

AUTHOR'S NOTE: Reeve learned that when he put his faith in God, he was provided with a life far better than the one he was living while using drugs. If you or one of your friends has a desire to turn away from drugs, I encourage you to talk with your parents, a counselor, or a pastor. You can also contact the National Youth Crisis Hotline at 1-800-HIT-HOME (1-800-448-4663) or the National Drug Abuse Hotline at 1-800-662-4357 for support services in your area.

. . . I STARTED PRAYING TO GOD FOR STRENGTH . . .

When I used to get teased, I always came back with a smart-aleck remark, making my bullies tease me even more. Every day was the same. I started getting really angry at them. I would get into fights and cause lots of trouble. I had no friends other than my twin sister. When we went into the seventh grade, I was still being picked on. I had made some friends, but they got picked on, too. Finally, I had had enough, so instead of getting angry and going right back at them, I started praying to God for strength so that I could resist my desire to fight them. And slowly, I found that His strength helped me face my tough days. Now, I use kindness rather than anger. It is amazing, but I don't get picked on as much anymore, and I have great friends!

DANITA, 14

SO WHEN YOU ARE TROUBLED . . .

When I was asked for my thoughts on the strength I find in God, they came from my heart in a poem. It goes like this:

God is my strength!

The strength to love
The strength to live
The strength to forget
The strength to forgive

Strength in numbers
Strength in pairs
Strength in friends
And the lives they share

We find strength
In every nook

In a family
Or in a book

But where does the original
Strength come from?
The strength to go on
When our hearts go numb?

"Who created
This strength?" you say
God Almighty
He helps us in every way

So when you are troubled
Do not shed a tear
Turn to Him for strength
And have no fear

SALEENA, 15

I WISH I COULD END THIS WITH "HAPPILY EVER AFTER" . . .

When I was ten years old, I couldn't have been happier. I was a carefree young girl just living my life. I was the child of divorced parents, but that didn't bother me because each of my families loved me equally, and I saw them both often. I went on Christmas vacations during the winter and to camps during the summer. I thought this was how life was supposed to be forever. As I grew older, I began to realize that problems do occur, and life isn't always easy. This realization came on a day that I will always remember clearly.

I was sitting in the kitchen at my dad's house, and he told me he needed to talk. I didn't know what about, but I said okay, and when I looked at him I knew that things were not okay. His face was very sad, and his eyes were filled with tears. He told me he had been diagnosed with something called ALS. It is a motor-neuron disease also known as Lou Gehrig's disease. He told me that there was no current cure and that the doctors had only given him two to five years to live. I felt like my world was crumbling. There wasn't anyone who could fix it, and no one who understood how I felt.

As time went on, I watched my dad, who had done a half–IronMan Marathon less than a year before, start walking with a cane. I watched my dad, who used to have a bowl of ice cream every night before bed, hardly eat at all and often have to spit into a cup because it was too hard to swallow. I watched my dad, someone who used to call me at least two times a week to check in, now have to get my stepmom to call while we talked on speaker phone because it was too hard to hold a long conversation because his speech had deteriorated so badly. I watched my dad, someone who used to fly his plane up to where I live to watch my brother and I play sports, not even be able to drive his car. I watched my dad go from being a big, strong, six-foot man, to being able to count almost all of his ribs. I watched my dad until he died.

Our only sense of peace was that we knew he was in heaven, and that he was out of his sick body and was happy. As time went on, I realized that I was not going to be able to get through the loss of my dad all by myself. I was going to need the support of my family, friends, and God. I felt that the only one who knew exactly how I felt was God. He had listened to all my thoughts and prayers throughout my dad's sickness and knew exactly what was in my heart. I knew He had heard everything and was going to continue to listen when I talked to Him. I know now that He gave me the strength to begin to overcome this difficult part of my life. I wish I could end this with "happily ever after," but that chapter in this story is yet to be experienced. Life isn't always like the story books that I read when I was ten years old. But I have learned that God will always be with me, no matter where life's journeys take me.

EMMA, 17

I WAS LOST IN WHO I WAS, WHO MY FAMILY WAS . . .

When my parents got a divorce, I became suddenly lost. I was lost in who I was, who my family was, who my leaders in life were. With encouragement from a friend, I went to a local youth group. It was only once a week and was for about two hours. Through the group, not only did I have time away from my family troubles, but time to be with God and find out who I really was as that was something I was really struggling with. I started praying every night. I prayed for His guidance and compassion. Slowly, I came to realize that things were getting easier and beginning to be okay. I don't know if it was just by chance that things got better when I started praying, but I really think it was because I let God know that I knew He was there, and I needed His love and guidance.

My parents' divorce has just become final. I know it will take a long time to get over it and accept everything that has gone on, and what my parents have done to each other and our family. But I think with time and the help of God, I will have the strength to make it through everything just fine and maybe come out a better person. If another teen asked me for the best piece of advice I could offer, I would have to say this: If you are trying to find out who you are, who you want to be, or where you are to go in life, go and find God and talk to Him. It is so easy, and He is always there for you. He understands what you are going through. He won't leave you like a friend might, and He is only a prayer away.

SUMMER, 14

WHEN WE DO NOT HAVE THE STRENGTH TO PICK UP OUR HEAD, GOD WILL HELP . . .

The dictionary defines strength as being "the power to resist force," but even the strongest man has emotional weaknesses. Many times we don't have enough strength to pull through the most emotionally straining times in our lives. Yet, God is there to guide us through these times. He knows that after persevering, struggling, and encountering hardships, these difficult life experiences will make us stronger in the future. This is not the physical strength described in *Webster's Dictionary*, but a strength defined with God's love and devotion to all of us. When we do not have the strength to pick up our head, God will help us gain enough strength to do so.

MICHAEL, 16

HE GIVES ME THE STRENGTH
TO FACE MY DAD . . .

Abuse. It is a scary and very real word to me. I am not saying that it happens all the time, but it does happen often. Sometimes it's not always physical abuse, but it's mental abuse, too. I think what hurts the worst is that I didn't do a thing to bring on my dad's anger. It's not so much the physical abuse that hurts; it's the mental abuse. It hurts me so deeply that I become very afraid of him. He has made me so insecure about myself that I have subconsciously put up a wall around me. There are only a few special people who have gotten through this shield, and God is one of them. He has gotten past the wall because He gives me strength, courage, and hope.

On the days that I just don't feel like living, He gives me the strength to do it. He gives me the strength to face my dad and the rest of the world. He gives me hope that maybe someday my dad will see how much he hurts me and stop the abuse. And maybe that will come sooner now because, most important, God gave me the strength to finally talk to someone about what my dad was doing. God just gives me so much that my dad doesn't or can't give me. That is one of the reasons He has gotten past my wall. I am very grateful to have God in my life. Amen!

YOLANDA, 14

AUTHOR'S NOTE: If you have ever found yourself in a situation like Yolanda's, please talk to a trusted adult. A teacher, school counselor, pastor, or family friend can guide you to seek help. You can also call the National Youth Crisis Hotline at 1-800-HIT-HOME (1-800-448-4663) or the National Clearinghouse on Child Abuse and Neglect at 1-800-394-3366 for guidance, support, and referrals. Know that no one deserves to be abused, and it is an individual's right as a human being to be safe. And when, like Yolanda, you just don't feel like living some days, please refer back to the "T" Talk in Chapter 3 for reassurance and guidance that suicide is not the answer. Seek comfort and courage from God, and find the strength in Him to talk to someone about what you are feeling.

. . . HIS STRENGTH CAN BE OUR STRENGTH . . .

"Put some muscle into that, boy!" "I expect you to have enough strength to lift that weight!" or "Put your back into it!" are all ways of saying that you need to put effort and strength into whatever you are doing. There are two different kinds of strength, though. There is man's strength, and then there is God's strength. God didn't intend for people to carry their burdens by themselves. God wants all of us to know that His strength can be our strength. When we dwell in God's strength, we receive grace, love, and forgiveness. God gives us strength in our lives when we face new challenges, when we doubt or are depressed. Often we can find His strength through prayer. When we pray, it gives God a chance to comfort us and guide us through our trials. So look to God for strength. He works in mysterious ways and will build you up when you are lifting a heavy load!

JASMINE, 14

"T" TALK

I am a very energetic and enthusiastic person. I have always loved challenging myself athletically. When I water-ski or play sports, I push myself to the limit. I suppose it is just my personality; I have an innate desire to compete, but even more important, I love to have fun! My husband is much the same way. Together we spend a great deal of time outdoors. With our children, we enjoy hiking, biking, and skiing. We also love to camp. When my daughter was a little over one and my son was three years old, my husband and I took them camping. The campground was dry and very dirty, but we had a fantastic time. I think our daughter ate more dirt that weekend than she did food! Little did I know that our fun-filled camping trip would change my life.

Over a month later, I began to feel sick. At first, I thought I had the flu. I was nauseous and fatigued. Throughout the next few months, I lost weight, muscle tone, and strength and experienced difficulty breathing. Anything that took muscle exertion left me breathless. As active as I normally was, I was devastated by my physical condition, and I was terrified that something was seriously wrong with me. I visited many doctors, but they were baffled by my condition. At one point, a specialist at a nationally acclaimed diagnostic institute patted me on the back and suggested that I was overstressed. I left there not knowing if I should cry and scream or commit myself to a psychiatric ward. People who know me call me an eternal optimist, but at that point I became depressed. I didn't have the strength to be the mom and wife I had always been, and no doctor could tell me what was wrong. I began to doubt myself and my symptoms.

Tragically, as my body deteriorated, I feared that I was dying. Finally, after six months, I saw another specialist who diagnosed me with Lyme disease, a bacteria that replicates as it invades your body systems and renders them useless. Apparently, a tick bit me when we were camping. The tick carried Lyme and passed it on to me. After five long years of treatment, I feel very blessed to be in excellent health today. Yet, I am also aware that my faith in God and my belief that He would be with me gave me the strength and courage to persevere. I am cognizant, too, of the many valuable lessons that God taught me through my illness. One encounter, in particular, reinforced the power of God's presence in my life.

It was a beautiful winter day as I traveled along a mountain road to meet my husband for lunch at a local ski resort. My body was quite weak and I had yet to be diagnosed, but I was grateful to be getting out and enjoying the day. As my children slept in the backseat, I drove along listening to the radio, when all of a sudden my right hand began to feel tingly, as if little needles were prickling my fingers and the palm of my hand. As the feeling progressed up my forearm, my fingers began to involuntarily curl into a tight fist. I began to feel afraid, not knowing what was happening to my body and very aware that if something happened to me, my kids would be alone and unprotected in the car. Suddenly, my right arm contracted and began to curl into my body. My left arm also began to follow the same pattern, tingling, contracting, and becoming useless. I feared that perhaps it was the altitude that was causing this episode, so I thought I should try to head back down the mountain. Even with the full use of one's hands, it would be a difficult turn to make under winter conditions. To my right was a huge wall of snow and to my left a sheer drop-off. Ice coated the road in an invisible sheet. But at that point, I felt that turning around was my only hope. I was beginning to feel the same tingling sensation in my face, and both of my hands now seemed glued to my chest. Without the benefit of my hands or forearms, I used my elbows and chest to turn my car around and guide it to the side of the road. I was unable to put my car into park and feared for my children's safety, sure that I would soon lose consciousness. With my foot on the brake, I waved my elbow out the window hoping someone would stop to help me, though no one did.

I was frustrated, helpless, and afraid when I realized I hadn't yet asked the only one who could help me. God knew my situation, and He was near. I prayed with all of my heart for God to give me the strength to hold on and to please have the next person stop. I also remember asking the Lord to let it be a good person, someone who would help me and protect my children. And He did. In fact, He sent two people in the next car. They reminded me of my parents, as the man got into my car and drove my children and me safely to an emergency room. His wife followed us and then made sure the kids were taken care of until my family arrived.

I later learned that the bacteria from the Lyme disease had attacked my respiratory system and ultimately caused that reaction in my body. But through that experience, the life lesson that I learned was most precious. I was reminded that God is always near, yet sometimes we forget to call on Him for help. He knows when we are afraid or hurting. If we turn to Him when we are troubled, He will comfort us with His strength.

Because I am a very independent person, I often try to control many situations in my life. Even when I am failing miserably, I stubbornly persist and usually watch things get worse. But when I let go and realize that, in fact, I don't have to be in control because God is, things seem to work out. It is difficult for Him to take care of me unless I allow Him to. Just like on the mountain, I couldn't make people stop to help me, but God could. I had to get beyond myself and my control to let God help me.

I don't believe that God caused my Lyme disease, but I do know that I have grown spiritually because of my encounter with Lyme. God has taught me and touched my life in so many ways through the disease, but when I was initially sick and undiagnosed, I couldn't see it.

I think that most people have experienced a time when life doesn't make sense. Have you experienced a trial in your life that left you feeling overwhelmed and unsure? Maybe like some of the teens who wrote for this chapter, your situation is severe and you feel as if your world has collapsed around you. What can you do? Rely on God's promise to pull you through. The Bible says that God is our rock, that if we rely on Him, He will be there. If we lay our fears and confusion on the foundation of God's love, He will give us the strength to persevere through our most challenging life situations. Do you remember the story from the Old Testament about David and Goliath? David knew that he could conquer Goliath because he understood that he would not face the giant alone. David knew with certainty that God would guide him and keep him safe. His courage flourished in the knowledge that God was with him.

If, like Yolanda, who shared her encounter with abuse, you, too, have had a similar experience, God can give you the strength to seek help. It is important that you do this because you do not in any way deserve to be abused. In fact, it is your right to be safe. It may be scary to reach out on your own for help, but with God beside you, you can do anything. Talk to an adult whom you trust, like a teacher, pastor, or school counselor. Let God take you by the hand and lead you there because you are His child, and He wants you to be safe. Let God pour courage upon your soul and give you the strength to protect yourself.

At the same time, perhaps the problems that you deal with in your life aren't extreme, like some of those you just read about. As a teacher and speaker, teens often come to me to talk about their problems and, although this chapter addresses very sensitive issues, most teenagers deal with dilemmas that are less intense. Many teens feel overwhelmed with school, sports, activities, or work. Others get disappointed with friendships or boyfriend/girlfriend relationships. Some teenagers feel frustrated when their parents don't seem to understand their problems or when their younger siblings invade their space. Perhaps you can relate to these issues. If so, please know that God is there to provide you with strength, too. The fact that your problem may not involve an extreme situation doesn't mean that you shouldn't call on the Lord for support and strength. The Bible tells us that God always wants us to call on Him. No problem is too big or too small for God because He loves us.

Extraordinarily, the power in His love breeds hope in our lives and gives us this strength. As a teen, your life can be very confusing, emotional, and lonely. It can also be fun, exciting, and filled with friends. Let God be one of your friends. Let Him share your life and bring you strength!

Mrs. T

Chapter Five

IN YOU I TRUST!

TRUSTING GOD IS THAT ESSENTIAL . . .

If you are reading this book in sequence and have just completed Chapters 3 and 4, then you know that various teens shared their most serious trials and tragedies. Although frequently people believe in God because they are brought up in a family of believers, sometimes it takes an extreme situation to lead others to their spiritual convictions. For these people, putting their trust in the Lord may be the only thing that gives them hope for their future. Trusting God is that essential. Throughout this chapter, teens share their philosophies of trust. You may be one who has put your trust in God since you were a young child. Or, perhaps, your relationship with God is recently evolving. Regardless, I believe you will find this chapter both enlightening and insightful. Take heart and trust in the Lord!

Mrs. T

I CAN TELL GOD
ANYTHING . . .

Throughout my life, I have always had a hard time trusting others—not because everyone in my life is not trustworthy, but because I have just been afraid to trust them. I am afraid of people breaking my confidence or making fun of me for what I have told them. Of course, throughout my life, I have found a few people I can trust, but there is only one I can trust completely—God. I know that whatever I have to say, He will listen to it, and whatever I have done, He will not make fun of me. I know that I will always be able to go to Him for help with anything. I do not have to worry about Him telling others. I can tell God anything, unlike with some of the people in my life, where I am only able to share some things with them. Being able to trust God completely has helped me greatly in my life. When there is no one in your life who you can talk to and trust, then all your feelings and emotions will just build up inside you, and this can cause many problems in your life. But if you are able to trust someone with anything you say or do, then it is easier to work out your problems. After I talk to God about something, I feel like I don't have to worry about it anymore. Many times, if you don't tell someone about something you may be worried about, then it will get even worse. Luckily, though, I have found that by talking to God about something, it makes it easier to deal with. I hope that for the rest of my life I will keep this complete trust that I have in God, and I hope that others will be able to find this trust in Him as I have.

BELINDA, 17

. . . IF THEY KNOW WHO I REALLY AM . . .

I don't trust people. I can't completely say why anymore. I think it's just out of habit. But it doesn't change the fact that I can't tell people how I really feel or who I really am. That no, everything is not okay, and I really just need a hug and a few nice words right now.

I'm afraid of what people will do if they know who I really am or how I really feel. I've seen so many other people do it. I've seen people tell a secret that literally moments before they promised to keep. I've seen people trash talk someone who was only a few feet away from them. I've seen people make promises that they never intended to keep.

I've just seen too many people betray another's trust. I can't help but think that those people, some who I call my friends, would do the same to me. And so I started to keep everything inside. Or I tried to. As time went on, I found it harder and harder each day. I began to search for an outlet. I tried writing in a journal, which helped, but only for a little while. All of my thoughts and feelings and secrets still seemed to be crushing me with their weight.

I'm not quite sure how I came upon God as an answer, but I eventually found myself praying to Him. The prayers were awkward at first. I wasn't quite sure what to say or how. And I didn't completely trust God either. But, over time, the mistrust went away. The prayers came to me easier and more often. And I felt like I could breathe again. I even feel like I can try to trust people again. I'm not there yet. I still freeze up a little when people ask me how I am and expect an honest answer. But it's a step—and one I made by learning to trust God.

ARIANE, 16

HE WILL NEVER LEAVE
MY SIDE . . .

Whenever anything isn't as good as I want it to be, such as my grades or my relationships with my parents or friends, I know that I can always turn to God. It often feels like I have nobody to trust when it comes to the problems in my life. But I do know that no matter what is going wrong or how bad things seem to get, I always can trust that God will be there. He will never leave my side, and for that, I am thankful.

DONNA, 15

I HAVE NO CLUE AS TO WHAT I WOULD BE LIKE . . .

Throughout my life, I have been guided to trust God. Today, I am old enough not to be guided anymore. I now *choose* to trust God. I trust God in many ways. I trust Him to guide me through my everyday life, to be there when I need comfort, and to direct me in doing what is right. Another simple reason why I put my trust in God is because I believe that He truthfully knows what is right for me. I have no clue as to what I would be like if I did not trust God. God has protected me from major injuries and drugs, and from me turning away from Him. He has taught me to love myself and, in doing so, I can share my love with other people. I have also learned to trust other people besides myself. I usually don't get on someone's bad side, but when I do, I turn to God and ask Him why I made that person angry. When I talk to God or pray to Him, I don't always hope for an answer. I hope that I can learn from my mistakes by talking them out with God. So, again I do trust God to be there when I am down or need to reason something out. He is an inspiration to me, and I look forward to the future because of my trust in Him.

DERECK, 16

. . . I CAN TELL HIM ANYTHING WITHOUT FEAR OF BEING JUDGED . . .

I think that teens have trouble putting their trust in other people. The main reason is mostly because of gossip and judgment. I trust in God, though. I know that He will never judge me, He will believe in me, and He will always look for the best in me. I don't have to lie to God about myself or pretend I'm someone I am not, like I do with some of my friends. I know He will always accept me for who I truly am. I know that I can trust God with anything and can tell Him anything without fear of being judged or pushed away. If everyone learned to trust God and His compassion, then maybe we could learn to trust each other more.

SANDRA, 14

. . . I FELT ABANDONED BY GOD . . .

I think when we become teenagers, life starts getting complicated. We wonder who we are. We know we need help, and we can't do it on our own. When I turned thirteen, life hit me in the face. The pressures of being a teen started to affect my relationships with my friends, my family, and more important, God! I felt like my family hated me, my friends were going their own way, and I couldn't find God anywhere. I started praying about it, but I felt like I was praying to a brick wall. So, I gave up all hope of a better life and relationship with God. Also, at the time, my best friend moved to Chicago. We had been friends for over half our lives, and I just couldn't let her go. I thought, *How could my life get any worse?* It got so out of hand that I thought about running away and never coming back. I was sad and angry with God. I stopped talking and listening to God altogether.

In the meantime, my church camp was coming up, and even though I had turned away from God, for some reason I really wanted to go. On the second day, the pastor was talking about God's love and hope when we feel abandoned. That was exactly what I was going through. I felt abandoned by God and everyone else. When I heard this message, I knew God was talking to me. I realized that I had shut Him out, not the other way around. He opened my eyes and my heart. God pulled me gently to my knees, and I was speechless. I just broke down in tears and poured my heart out to God. I never felt so loved and touched in my life! From then on, I knew God would always be there for me. I trust Him and know that He loves me and will never leave me. Now, when I pray, I know He is listening to everything.

If you are reading this and you feel abandoned, know that God has never left. Open your heart and let Him come in! God is there. I know He is! Trust Him! He won't leave, I promise!

KERAN, 14

. . . TRUST HIM TO LEAD YOU . . .

I'm a shy and quiet person, so when I started my fresh-man year in high school, I was scared. I didn't have any really good friends from my previous school, and I had no idea who to hang out with. For about two weeks, I just floated around, sometimes hanging out with acquain-tances from my old school. I never really considered that God might have a part in helping me find a group to hang out with, but now that I look back on it, I truly believe that He did. During the first week of school, an old friend intro-duced me to a redheaded girl. She seemed nice at the time, but I had no idea who she hung out with or if she was even the kind of person I wanted to be influenced by. Toward the end of the second week of school, I saw her standing in the hallway alone, so I went up and started talking to her. Because God gave me the courage to talk to her, I found a great friend who is still my friend today. As I was talking to her, the group of friends that she hung out with walked up. She introduced me to them, and they accepted me for who I was. I realized afterward that God must have been leading me in this direction because none of these people were in any of my classes, so there was no way for me to get to know them. God can work in your life in many different ways. You just have to trust Him to lead you where He wants you to be. I'm glad that I followed His lead!

KAJ, 15

. . . "Look, Mommy, she has one leg" . . .

I was born different from everyone else, but I know who I am, and I trust God to show me the way. I think my poem, "I Am," explains it best:

I am loving and kind.
I wonder why people think that I'm different from them
    because I am not.
My difference just shows.
I hear little kids say, "Look, Mommy, she has one leg."
I see all the little eyes staring at me and little fingers
    pointing at me.
I want for everyone not to care what I look like.
I am loving and kind.

I pretend not to hear them say the things
    they say.
I feel sad that they don't know that what is on the
    inside is what counts.

I touch the sweaty handles of my crutches every day.
I worry that no one will like me at first sight.
I cry sometimes when I feel sad about the way
  I am,
Wishing everyone would see me as God does.
I am loving and kind.

I understand the way God made me.
I trust that God put me on this Earth for some reason
  and
If it takes a lifetime, I'm going to find out why.
I am loving and kind.
I trust God.
I have hope.

LENNA, 15

I HAVE NEVER DONE ANYTHING TO CAUSE MY PARENTS' DOUBT . . .

No one ever said that being a teen was easy, but I never expected it to be this hard. I never expected a lot of things, least of all a lack of trust from my parents. It's tough to deal with. Authority is necessary, but it can also be frustrating. I have never done anything to cause my parents' doubt, and yet I am still treated with no trust. This tells me that they do not respect how I feel about things. In another sense, however, I can see where they are coming from. I can understand their need to keep me close by them. After all, I will be leaving home for college in a few years, and they don't want to see me get hurt. Oddly enough, when I feel too stifled or mistrusted by my parents, I feel that I can turn to God and be trusted. I know deep inside that He trusts me and my judgment. He guides me, as well, and it is because of Him that I am able to trust that everything will work itself out.

JAQULIN, 14

. . . INSIDE I WAS STILL REGRETTING IT A LITTLE . . .

I have always been taught to look to God and trust Him when I am confused. Well, in August of last year, my great-grandmother was starting to get sick, and I looked to God for guidance.

Grandma Chris was ninety and lived in a home for the elderly in our town. My grandparents (she was my grandpa's mom) went to see her daily, and we went at least once a week between sports practices for my brother and me. My great-grandma was full of spunk and spirit in her old age. One of her favorite things was to knit and paint pottery for my cousins and me. I had so many painted trinkets that I didn't know what to do with them.

Anyway, one day after practice my mom told me that Grandma Chris had to go to the hospital. She had to have surgery and was having trouble breathing. I really thought that she would pull through. But as the days went on, she had to rely on a breathing tube, and she only got worse instead of better. Every time we thought she was getting better, she would slip back down.

Each night, I would pray to God that she would use all

of her strength and pull through for us. Then one night my brother told my parents that he thought he needed to see her if this was the end. It was late, the hospital was an hour away, and I had a big basketball game the next day. My mom came into my room and asked me if I wanted to go, too. All I could say was I didn't know. I wondered if I would ever see my great-grandma again, but to see her in the hospital with tubes down her throat? I thought back to my last memory of her. I had picked her up for church with my grandma, and I remembered seeing the biggest smile on her face because we were there.

I finally decided not to go with them, but inside I was still regretting it a little. A few days later, she passed away. I was listening to my mom, aunt, and grandparents talk about how she was so miserable in the hospital. It hurt them to see her in so much pain. I kept remembering the way I saw her that day before church, a smile from ear to ear and so happy. That's when I realized that God had helped me make my decision. Why should my last memory of my Grandma Chris be of her in pain? It was the right thing not to go see her. I'm glad that I trusted the memories and feelings God gave me about what I should do that night. If you are ever in a hard place, trust God to guide you. Even if it is not a direct answer, He will help you, just like He did for me.

DJ, 14

. . . I KNOW I CAN TRUST GOD . . .

Even though I can't see Him, I know I can trust God. He listens to me and doesn't make judgments. He hears what I say and just lets me talk. Sometimes it's a big comfort to know that the person you're pouring your heart out to won't give you a lecture or think you're weird.

RILEY, 15

. . . JUST LET GO OF
THE ROPE . . .

A few years ago, we were at a lake, and I was learning how to water-ski behind my uncle's boat. Despite the in-depth instructions that my uncle and cousins had given me, I still felt nervous. I was an okay swimmer, but I hated not doing well at something. I remember getting myself in position and my uncle taking off. For a few seconds, I was able to get up on the skis behind the boat and felt that I was getting the hang of it. *Easy*, I thought. Suddenly, I crossed my skis, lost my balance, and fell. I hit the water, shocked that I hadn't completed the task. My mind went blank. What was I supposed to do? What had my uncle and cousins said to do if I fell? All I could think of doing was to hang on to the rope as if it was my lifeline. As my uncle continued to drive the boat, I clutched the rope, afraid if I let go I would end up slamming into the boat engine or drowning. My mind raced with crazy thoughts of dying and of all the things I had not done yet. I could do nothing but cling to the rope in complete terror. Suddenly, I heard a kind voice in my head. This voice calmly told me to let go of the rope. I thought to myself, *There is no way I am going to let go of this rope. I will die.* The voice again calmly told me to just let go of the rope. I thought, *No way. I don't want to die.* For a third time, I heard the voice, "Trust in Me. Let go of the rope." At that exact moment, I felt a sense of calm sweep over my body. I knew that if I trusted in God, everything would be all right. I just needed to let go of the rope and trust in Him. I did exactly that. I trusted in God and let go of the rope. I didn't crash into the boat engine, and I didn't die. In fact, I dog-paddled while my uncle turned the boat around to pick me up.

Although this happened years ago, there are still times in my life that I feel I can't let go of the rope. Being a teenager is full of stress. Sometimes, this stress is so overwhelming that I don't feel as if I can handle it. Starting high school, changing schools, moving, family crises, peer pressure—the list goes on. I become overwhelmed thinking about what others will think, how I will succeed, what I am supposed to do, and so on. I tighten my grip on the rope that connects me to my insecurities and fear. Just as I think I can't let go, I remember the voice from the day on the lake telling me to trust and let go. By praying and trusting in God that He will do what is best and guide me to make the right decisions, I can let go and stop worrying about what my peers will think or if I fit in or what will happen in stressful situations. I can allow the calmness and peace to flow over me once more. All it takes is letting go and trusting God.

KHRISTOPHER, 14

"T" TALK

One morning, Sarah [not her real name] came into my classroom sobbing uncontrollably. She could hardly catch her breath as she tried to speak to me through her tears. Her parents had broken the news to her just an hour before that they were filing for divorce. Sarah just didn't understand. They were the perfect family; everybody had always teased her about that. They had never had any problems. She rarely, if ever, saw them argue. So why would they be getting a divorce?

Apparently, her mom had fallen in love with another man. She was moving out and leaving Sarah, her little sister, and her dad to live with this man. Sarah could not believe that her mom would betray her dad this way. But what hurt more was that she felt her mom had deceived her, too. Isn't it just a given, Sarah asked me, that every teenage girl should have a mom there to talk to? How could her mom choose another man over her family? Sarah had always naturally trusted that her mom would be there for her. How could she just walk away? Now, she didn't know if she could ever trust again.

Sarah's story is not uncommon. Many teens have experienced situations in which someone has shattered their trust. Trust is a fragile bridge that brings people together. But because it is delicate, it can easily be destroyed. Unfortunately, when this happens, it often leaves people hanging on by a thread, feeling confused, hopeless, and sometimes even angry.

Have you ever felt like you're barely holding on, shocked by a betrayal? Perhaps, like Sarah, you had always believed that your parents would stay committed to each other and remain the foundation for your family. Yet, here they are, divorcing. Or maybe it is your friends who broke your trust. Suppose they betrayed your confidence or talked about you behind your back. If such an incident has occurred in your life, it might be difficult for you to trust again. Many teens have told me, "Mrs. T, I am not going to let myself get burned twice." They feel that it is easier to stay away from friendships or guard their emotions around family members, rather than set themselves up for heartache. The sadness in this philosophy is that in choosing not to trust, teens risk missing out on love and joy, friendships and fun.

Or sometimes it goes much deeper. Take the two students who entered their school, shot several of their classmates and a teacher, then killed themselves. Apparently, they felt betrayed as a result of years of being teased and taunted, and they began to isolate themselves. They trusted no one. It makes me so sad to think that if there had been just one person they could have trusted enough to talk to, perhaps the senseless and tragic murders could have been prevented.

In all the years that I have worked with teenagers, one

issue that continues to recur is the concept of trust. Teens talk about trust as a value that they hold very close to their hearts. They treasure trust and do anything possible to protect it. If someone damages or deceives this trust, it is as if they are breaking the person's heart. You may have experienced this type of betrayal and know what it feels like. As much as your parents, siblings, or friends may not intend to break your heart or shatter your trust, occasionally it happens. During these times you may feel as if you can trust no one. Well, take heart! There is someone you can always trust: God. He never turns away from you or breaks His promises. God is always listening and constantly available. At times when we feel so alone, all we have to do is call on Him, and He is there.

I often think about the disciples when they were out on the sea in their little fishing boat. A storm came from out of nowhere as it often does at sea. They were so afraid. I would guess that they felt helpless and alone. And then, without fail, up walks Jesus. Yes, you read it right. They were in the middle of the sea, and here came Jesus walking on water, calming not only the sea, but the disciples' fears, as well. I'm sure that once they realized it was really Him and He had come to save them, they must have asked themselves, "Why didn't we trust? He told us He would always be here. He asked us to trust Him, so why didn't we?"

My parents experienced a similar situation. They were in their sailboat, sailing south toward Mexico, when they encountered a storm. The waves were huge, and my mom and dad were still inexperienced sailors. It was my mom's turn on night watch, and she was terrified. Yet, in the midst of the storm, God was near. My mom prayed throughout her watch, but as the storm grew, she felt that her prayers came secondary to her fright. After two hours, my dad took over watch, and my mom went below. She tried to get some rest, but as she listened to the sounds of the water crashing against the hull, panic set in, and she imagined the boat breaking into little pieces, leaving her and my dad to drown.

So, she continued to pray. As her fear heightened, my mom began to realize that she had absolutely no control of their current situation. She couldn't calm the storm. She had no authority over the ocean as it thrashed their vessel from wave to wave. Only in that moment did she understand that she had to completely surrender her usual need for control and put her trust in God. She prayed, "Okay, God, I'm afraid, and I'm not able to feel brave, so please take care of the sea and calm it down."

As Jesus demonstrated with the disciples, He has the power to do such things. Within moments of my mom's prayer, the noise of the storm began to quiet, and the relentless waves became still. My mom has always believed in the influence of prayer, but this absolute and virtually immediate response from God caused her to feel humble and appreciative of His power. He calmed my mother's fears, as well as the sea, and reminded her that although some situations will be out of her control, if she chooses to trust God, He will be there.

Like my mom, many of us have the need to control various circumstances in our lives. We like to take hold of the reins and assert direction and command. This gives us a sense of order that makes us feel safe and secure. However, when things happen in our lives that cause the reins to be ripped from our hands, it creates chaos and confusion within us.

This is why it is so important to place our trust in God. When it comes right down to it, He is truly the one in control. When we try to dominate every facet of our lives, we are, in essence, trying to dominate God. Eventually, though, instead of feeling peaceful, we will feel frustration, disappointment, or anger when circumstances don't turn out as we've planned. Yet, if we set our daily worries and blessings at God's feet and choose to trust in Him, He promises to guide and comfort us.

Jesus makes this commitment to you, personally. He only asks that you trust Him. Let Him calm your fears and still your storms. God is with you always. If you "let go, and let God," as the old saying goes, or "just let go of the rope," as Khristopher learned to do, God will direct your path and never leave you alone. Without a doubt, there will be situations in your life that are completely out of your control, as Sarah learned when her mother left. Although she couldn't change the current upheaval in her family, if she had let go and let God comfort her, she may have felt more peace.

In addition, if you have difficulty trusting others, I pray that when you experience the peacefulness and comfort that fills your heart when you trust in the Lord, you will have the confidence to trust others as well. With God by your side, I pray that you will open your heart and experience the love and joy that relationships can bring when you entrust yourself to others. I think you may find that when you do this, they will trust you as well. It is a wonderful feeling and a valuable gift. God will help you along the way; just put your trust in Him. Lord, in You I trust!

Mrs. T

Chapter Six

GOD, HOW COULD YOU LET THIS HAPPEN?!

. . . GOD IS WAITING

PATIENTLY . . .

Have you ever asked God, "How could you let this happen?" I know many teenagers, as well as adults, who have. Sometimes situations occur in our lives that we don't understand. They can leave us feeling confused, frustrated, or even angry. Occasionally, people blame God for the injustices or cruelties of life. I included this chapter in *Teens Talkin' Faith* because I wanted you to know that if you have ever felt angry at God, you are not alone. You will find teen contributors who share that they have felt much the same way. However, I also want you to recognize that God is waiting patiently and lovingly for you to realize that blaming Him for life's tragedies or frustrations is not the answer. Instead, when you turn to God for guidance and reassurance, He will open your heart and your eyes to understanding, acceptance, and hope.

Mrs. T

HOW CAN A MOTHER, WHO HAS CARED FOR HER CHILD FOR TEN YEARS, JUST WALK AWAY . . .

The events of that Sunday morning in March are still fresh in my mind. We had gone to church like always, where my mom was my Sunday schoolteacher. On this particular Sunday, a friend of mine had come with us. The details aren't so important, but I remember that the car ride home seemed to take forever. I remember a lot of screaming and yelling between my mom and my dad, and a lot of curse words, too. After that car ride, my mom was gone. I was ten years old, but my mother was gone and starting a new life without me. How can a mother, who has cared for her child for ten years, just walk away one day? I still don't know.

That was a very traumatic day for me. It turned my life upside-down. I was really depressed, as were my dad and sister. So as my only remaining family, they couldn't help me. My friends, who were as young and naive as I was, had no idea what to say. I was alone, so I turned to God. The hurt wouldn't go away, though. I prayed and prayed, but I was still alone. That's when I stopped depending on God. He let me down. He let something bad happen to me. My faith went straight down the tubes. I was so mad at God. I got new friends who were in the same parental situation as I was in, and I stopped believing. For three years, I was Godless. Whether it was puberty, a new school, or my faithlessness, I had a whole new personality. I changed so much, and mostly for the worst. I didn't go to church in those three years, nor did I pray. I was lost, and I really didn't care.

But then last year, I realized that my new life was failing me. It left me empty inside. Slowly, I began to have a desire to find God again. Recently, I have been more complete than since my mom left. It has been a long journey, but I am glad I am not mad at God anymore and that I have Him in my life again.

SHANE, 15

. . . MY LIFE CAME CRASHING
TO A HALT . . .

I remember thinking my life was about to be ruined when my parents delivered the "big news." At that point, I thought God had made a terrible mistake. For all of my life, we had lived in our native country. My whole life was there—my family and friends, my school and my church. I had always imagined us as the family that would never move. That is why, when my mom and dad told my little brother and I that we were leaving, my life came crashing to a halt. The fact that we were leaving our country, too, made it hurt that much more. I was really angry with God at that point. I have heard the sayings, "You can't always get what you want" and "Life isn't always fair," but this was just ridiculous. I felt like God had deserted me. I asked Him, "Why have You abandoned me?"

Too soon, we were packed and ready to hit the agonizingly long journey ahead of us. I really was not looking forward to our new life. Throughout that summer, many thoughts ran through my head. I thought I would never forgive God for this event in my life. I thought I would never see my friends again, and I was sure I was in for the worst.

Once school started, I began to loosen up. The teachers were great, my classmates were nice, and I was actually happy. After getting to know my current best friend, I started feeling guilty for feeling happy because of how mad I had been at God for moving my family. I realized then that God knew I would adapt to my new environment. I know that He has forgiven me for not trusting Him. It was all in His plan for my family and me. This time has become one of the best in my life! I have started high school now, and I love it. What I also love is that my family has never been this close. I have learned that sometimes in life, God might change it up a bit. Instead of getting angry, I should have been patient, because it all turned out wonderfully in the end.

GEMMA, 14

MY HEART BREAKS OVER
MY DAD . . .

There was a day this past summer that I will remember for all of my life. My mom explained to me that my dad had cancer. My immediate response was, "There is no God! Where did You go? Why did You let this happen to me?" I was so angry with Him.

As days passed, and I saw my family begin to deal with this diagnosis, I started to see the many blessings in my life. I witnessed my mother's amazing love for my father, and I saw the medical community work to help my father get the tests he needed and begin treatment. Friends and family began to show their support and love. Cards and prayers of support were overwhelming. We received a letter from someone we didn't even know. She heard about my dad and wanted us to know that she would pray for him. What unbelievable, unconditional love! I believe now that this love came from the hand of God.

The diagnosis came right before I was to begin my freshman year at a new school that my parents and I were passionate about me attending. As I prepared for school, I realized that God has never left me. He has been by my side all along, even before my dad's cancer. You see, the past four years my dad has been the one to stay home with me. God blessed me with that. He was with my family when He blessed my mom with the talents and courage that she has to take care of our family. Also, now that I am a student at my new school, I feel supported every day. As I think about these things, I realize there are no coincidences. There is a plan, though sometimes painful, but if we remain faithful and quiet, we will hear the voice of God telling us that He is with us.

For me to have remained angry would have overshadowed all the wonderful things that are my life—the life that God gave me and the plan that He has for me. My heart breaks over my dad, but I know I would rather go through this pain than to never have known or felt my dad's love. With that in mind, as it says in the Bible, I lean on, trust in, and am confident in the Lord, with all of my heart and mind, and I do not rely on my own insight or understanding. Instead, I try to follow Proverbs 3:5–6, "Trust in the Lord with all your heart and lean not on your own understanding; in all your ways acknowledge Him, and He will make your paths straight."

LUKE, 14

I BLAMED GOD FOR
ALL THE PAIN . . .

I think God is patient because every time something goes bad or wrong, I usually get angry. When I was little, I would blame God for all the bad and depressing times. I was often depressed and sad because I was adopted when I was a baby, and I just didn't quite fit in all that well. I had some kids whom I was close to, but it was hard for me to make many friends. Some people made fun of me because of my race, which didn't make it any easier. I blamed God for all the pain and hurt I had to go through, but later I began to trust Him. Sometimes, I still get depressed, but I just think of all the good things. For example, today I have a loving family, good friends, a house, and lots of other good things to come.

RAGENA, 14

. . . *I GOT MAD AT GOD AND STOPPED PRAYING* . . .

As I lay in bed thinking about tomorrow, I hear the front door shut. In walks my brother, drunker than ever. He is so loud that he wakes up my parents. I hear them yelling at each other. Then he says something mean and walks out the door. I hear my mom start to cry. Every night we go through the same thing over and over again. Sometimes the pain of knowing what he is doing to himself and the danger he is putting himself in is unbearable. All I want to do is lock myself in my room and cry. But I don't. I somehow get through it. If only he knew that every night he doesn't come home, I expect a phone call from the hospital telling us that he is in critical condition. I couldn't stand to live without him. He had been my role model for so many years, but then he began to change.

About a year ago, I began to pray every night for him, and every Sunday that I went to church I prayed for him. One night, I thought to myself, *This isn't working; what good is this doing?* So I got mad at God and stopped praying, but things only got worse. So I decided that maybe, just maybe, if I started praying again, it would get better slowly.

Well, ever since I have been praying again, things have gradually gotten better. Before, my brother didn't even take the word "job" to mind, and now he has one. Even though he still drinks, I think he is getting much better. I used to not believe that God would actually listen to what I had to say, but now I know that He does and He will help. I just hope that one day my brother will see that his drinking is not the way and that he will get some serious help. I can only pray that this day will be soon. God has given me the strength and the hope to deal with my brother and help him through these times. Sometimes I think that when my brother looks at me, he wants to stop drinking, but he can't because he has gotten himself hooked. I pray that he will find God someday and understand what he is putting himself and our family through.

STEPHANIE, 14

. . . I ACTUALLY BECAME A PRETTY HARDCORE ATHEIST . . .

My life has been rather different from that of the ordinary American teenager. I was born in South Korea and lived in Pakistan and Russia before settling down in the United States. My father was the CEO of a large company for much of Europe and Asia, and as such, I had no material desires and not much strife. It wasn't the stereotypical boyhood, filled with Americana, dogs, and bike rides, but it was by no means unhappy. All in all, as a young boy I felt very secure. However, it is precisely when you think that all is going well that things seem to come crashing down around you.

I didn't have too much of a relationship with God. I went to church every Sunday because my parents wanted me to, I liked the music, and I thought the wine tasted kind of funny. But I was still too young to have a deep emotional connection. Therefore, when my dad declared a family meeting one day and spoke the fateful word "divorce," instead of turning to God for strength and support, I turned away. I cursed Him. I hated Him. For a boy of ten, life had suddenly lost all meaning. With my dad no longer in the family, our main economic resource was lost, so my mother, my sister, and I were forced to leave Moscow and move to the United States. From the life of economic ease that I had come to expect, I suddenly moved into a smaller house, attended a public school, and experienced problems I hadn't had before. Throughout all of this, the only role God played for me was that of a scapegoat, someone I could blame for my new hardships. I seemed to hunt for reasons why He couldn't exist, and I actually became a pretty hardcore atheist. After a few years, my mother remarried, and we moved again. I entered a local middle school there, and I quickly turned depressive and suicidal. Finally, I told my mom of all the problems I was having, and we decided to make a rather ironic decision—for an atheist, that is. We decided that I should leave my secular public school for a private Christian school. Understandably, this rather forced me to reconsider God for the first time in years. It also gave me the chance to look at the person I was and how much I had changed from the happy child I had been before the divorce. It took me most of middle school to make this realization, so I entered high school with the resolution to change and begin with a clean slate. I wanted to live by Scripture and be a good person. The final nail on my atheistic coffin occurred when I went on a school retreat. The love and support I felt there convinced me that God existed and actually had my best interest in mind. After a lot more reflection, I realized that my ordeal had taught me many things about life and proper living. From a spoiled child, I became a man. Although I will readily admit that my trial pales in comparison with others, the lessons learned are just as applicable. God stood by me, loved me, and knew that I would someday stand on my own two feet and thank Him for allowing me to suffer. For in my hardships, I found God.

DONAVAN, 17

. . . I FOUND MYSELF DOUBTING GOD AND BEING VERY ANGRY . . .

My faith in God has always been an important factor in my life, and it has always been very strong. However, last year my beliefs were put to a test. Twelve years of religious school could not prepare me for the gravest experience of my life. Last year, a week before Thanksgiving, my cousin committed suicide. He was sixteen years old, the same age as me. His death came as a complete shock to my entire family. Even though my faith had always been strong, I found myself doubting God and being very angry with Him. I couldn't believe that the same God who had delivered so many blessings to me previously could tear my life apart by taking someone I loved away from me at such a young age. This was a very difficult, stressful time in my life. I am very lucky to have a family, teachers, and friends who have been supportive through this time. Through a lot of thinking and prayer, my faith in God has been restored. I still feel anger when I think about my cousin, but I have grown to understand that God was not punishing me, and I need His guidance and support to get through these tough times.

JILLIAN, 17

AUTHOR'S NOTE: Remember, if you or someone you know is contemplating suicide, it is so important to reach out for help. Jillian's cousin made a choice to take his own life. It was a choice he didn't have to make. Parents, pastors, counselors, teachers, or family friends would be the best people to talk to, or you could call the National Suicide Hotline at 1-800-SUICIDE (1-800-784-2433).

. . . *I DIDN'T UNDERSTAND WHY HE HAD TO TAKE AWAY MY MOTHER* . . .

When I was little, I knew about God, but I thought the only reason people prayed to Him was when they needed help. I never knew that you could just pray to Him if you were having a bad day and needed someone to listen. I would pray about things like making up with friends after a fight or finding a lost pet. I always made up with friends and I always found my lost pet, so I thought that God was the greatest. Then, when my mom died about four years ago, I was angry with God because I didn't understand why He had to take away my mother. It wasn't fair that all my friends had moms and I didn't. I didn't think that He was the greatest, and I never prayed anymore.

Four years later, I started to talk to someone about my mom's death because I was having a hard time with it. She asked me about my faith, and I had no answer. I mean, I still believed in God and heaven, but it wasn't the same as when I was little. I think I was still really mad at Him. She brought up faith a lot, though, and I always felt weird because I hadn't thought about it in a long time. Then when she said she would pray for me, it made me think, *Why couldn't I pray for myself?* I started to pray to God and asked Him to help me. After that, I felt a little bit more reassurance and comfort. So, I started to pray more often. It started to feel really good. I stopped praying to Him only for help and started just to talk and tell Him what was going on in my life. Although I still miss my mom, I am not angry anymore because now I know God is the greatest!

MARISSA, 15

. . . GOD WAS CARRYING IT
FOR ME . . .

Anger is a natural feeling that every person experiences at one time or another. Sometimes we let our anger affect the things that mean the most to us. I remember a point in my life when it seemed like everything that could go wrong did. My best friend was moving away, some close family members were moving too, and a friend of mine took his own life. I was feeling down and very angry at God. It was as if God had gone on a long coffee break and had lost track of time. I didn't know what to do. Every time I turned to God for answers, something would happen to make the bond between God and me just a little bit weaker. I could not stop thinking that maybe God had just forgotten about me or maybe He did not want me anymore. Had I done something wrong that would make God turn away from me? I needed to find some answers, so I decided to go to my room and just sit and pray. After every time I did this, it seemed like the burden on my shoulders got lighter and lighter. Eventually, it was as if God was carrying it for me. Everything seemed right again. I guess the coffee break was over!

WINN, 17

MY BROTHER WAS ARRESTED
TWICE MORE . . .

My older brother and I had been pretty close. We used to go to youth group and just hang out. I had always been very strong in my faith and had recently been baptized. One night, I was holding my brother's jacket when a packet of cigarettes fell out. I was shocked. I wondered why my brother was smoking and why he was hiding it. After that, my brother started getting into bad stuff. I asked God to help my brother to stop and to help me be strong. On my brother's seventeenth birthday, he went out with some friends. My parents asked him to be home by 11:00. At two in the morning, I heard my mom crying. I got up, and she told me that my brother had been arrested for use of marijuana, driving under the influence, and curfew violation. I was so upset. How could God let this happen to him? I wondered how He could let my brother do something so bad.

After that, I started to get mad at God, and I turned away from Him. My brother was arrested twice more. I was so mad at God, I could barely stand it. Then I started talking to my youth pastor. He helped me to realize that maybe God was showing me that sometimes people just make poor choices and that these choices have consequences. I then understood that this is why my brother had been arrested, and it wasn't God's fault. I learned that God didn't deserve my blame, and I began to trust Him again.

DANIELLE, 14

"T" TALK

The summer of Amanda's eighth-grade year was awe-some. She and her friends spent tons of time together, and they always had fun. Her family was close, and she got along with her parents remarkably well. But what inspired Amanda most that summer was her relationship with God. She said, "It was the best!" Anytime she was alone, she spent time talking to God. Amanda loved to pray and delighted in her weekly youth group. She valued her faith, her family, and her life.

But when school started, Amanda's perspective shifted. She said everything changed—her looks, personality, friends, family, and especially her relationship with God. Amanda felt that her friends had turned on her, and rumors were being spread about her that weren't true. To compound that, school was more difficult than it had been in the past, and her grades dropped. It seemed like everybody was on her case, especially her parents, and Amanda began to feel that her life was worthless. As the stresses in her life became overwhelming, Amanda turned away from God. Instead of spending her time alone, praying as she had done in the past, Amanda became consumed with thoughts of suicide. Each night she would think about how she would end her life, telling herself that everyone would be happier if she was gone. She knew deep down that suicide wasn't the answer to her problems, but she was so focused on herself and her needs that she couldn't see beyond to the hope of the future.

In addition, she blamed the one to whom she later realized she should have been turning. Amanda was intensely angry with God. She accused Him repeatedly, saying, "God, why do You let me feel this hurt? Why are You doing this to me? I can't believe You, God. All my problems are Your fault!" As Amanda's anger at God grew, so did her plans to take her life. On the night that she had promised herself she would end her life, Amanda was alone in her room. Suddenly, she felt someone grab her, but when she turned to see who it was, no one was there. With that, she fell to the floor, sobbing. Amanda finally understood that she didn't want to end her life; she just wanted her problems to go away. Mostly, Amanda felt enlightened by an unfailing belief that it was God who stopped her. Amanda eventually realized that God was with her the whole time. He didn't want her to die, and He knew that deep down inside she didn't want to take her life either.

Amanda came to understand that had she turned to God with her problems instead of blaming Him for the trials in her life, He could have guided and comforted her. Amanda's youth pastor helped her to understand that it wasn't God who had turned on her; it was Amanda who had shut herself off from God. Yet, God accepted Amanda's anger. Perhaps He shows such mercy because He can identify. Remember the account in the gospel where Jesus goes into the temple of God and overturns the tables of those who were using such a holy place to buy and sell goods? When I think of someone overturning tables, I imagine rage. I assume Jesus was angry that the house of His Father was being used for trade instead of prayer, worship, and healing. So, although Amanda shunned God and placed the anger toward her life situation on Him, God understood. He waited patiently while Amanda figured this out, and, as she learned, He never left her side.

Perhaps you have experienced a time in your life when you have been angry with God. If so, know that you are not alone. Like any situation in which there is pain and heartache, it is typical to try to place the blame for the injustice on a specific entity. Often, that entity is God. It is quite common to blame God for life's inequities. After all, we frequently blame Him because we believe in Him. The wonderful thing about God is that He loves us so much that He is willing to take the blame. But, really, He doesn't deserve it. It is true that there are many things that happen in our lives that don't seem fair. For example, if someone we love gets cancer, it just doesn't seem right. We feel fearful and angry, and God is a perfect target for our outrage. However, I don't believe He caused the cancer. Nor do I presume that God wants to see us in physical or emotional pain. I do believe, though, that our time on this Earth is a personal and spiritual journey in which we grow from everything that we experience. I think that God can use the situations in our lives to teach us valuable lessons.

For example, during spring break of my sister Jaime's

sophomore year in college, she and some classmates traveled to Mexico for a week of missionary work. They had worked all year planning for the event and were very excited. Following their arrival, they worked together the first few days to build homes for people who lived there, in addition to providing other missionary services. Each morning they would get up, share a breakfast together, and then pile into the few cars they had to get to the worksites. In the small amount of spare time they had, they took time to pray, sing praises, and have fun! One day, while traveling to that day's destination, one of the vehicles carrying five students was hit head-on by another car. Three kids were killed. These teenagers were on a mission, doing God's work, and they were killed. It just didn't make sense to me. My sister and the others spent the next few days dealing with the tragedy and finishing their work.

When I spoke with Jaime after the accident, I asked her if she was mad at God. I felt mad at Him, and I didn't even know these kids. Why not be angry? They were in Mexico doing missionary work. How could God let them die? What kind of thanks is that? Of course, I just assumed that my sister would be angry, too. But she had a different perspective. She said that they had all experienced a variety of feelings, but anger was not one of them. More than anything, Jaime said, there was an overwhelming sense of mercy and compassion that encircled them. They had come to Mexico to help several families build homes. Yet after the accident, it was the families they had come to help who comforted, supported, and guided them. Roles reversed, and despite the sadness and grief experienced by all, love and compassion prevailed. As tragic as the accident was, God was able to teach the missionary students a valuable life lesson through the kindness of the Mexican families.

Frequently, though, when such tragedies happen, it is easier to blame God than to try to understand what can be learned from the situation. It is important to know, however, that anger often is just a variable mask that guards our heart from the fear, confusion, or sadness that is lingering in our midst. Sometimes it is simpler to get angry than to accept other such emotions that hurt so deeply. Eventually, though, it is important that we identify what we are actually feeling so we can deal with those emotions and learn from our life experiences. Part of God's awesome humility is demonstrated when He accepts our misplaced anger and patiently waits for us to figure out what we are truly feeling.

Finally, when we stop being angry at God, we can open our hearts to His guidance, and with His help we can deal with our adversities. Like Amanda learned, when we lose perspective and become consumed with anger, sometimes it is essential to seek the guidance of someone who can give us a new outlook. In addition to God, Amanda's youth pastor helped her see her situation in a different light. Pastors, as well as parents, teachers, friends, counselors, or any trusted adult, can provide objective guidance that may redirect our thoughts, lighten our load, and give us a more positive attitude.

It is also essential to understand that, although it may be normal to blame God or become angry with Him, we should ask ourselves, "What kind of choice was made that led to this ultimate outcome?" For instance, perhaps someone chose to drink before they got behind the wheel of a car, resulting in a fatal accident. This type of situation isn't

God's fault; it is a human choice. Yet even if the fault lies with a specific individual, if we harden our hearts and become angry and unforgiving, the one we hurt the most is ourselves. I suppose we hurt God, too, because there is no room for love in anger and blame. God tells us in the Bible that without love, we are nothing. He says that love bears all things, believes all things, hopes all things, and endures all things. I pray that in the future, when you feel angry, you will open your heart to God and let His love fill your soul.

                                                          Mrs. T

AUTHOR'S NOTE: If needed, please take time to turn to Appendix II at the end of the book for additional referral services for grief and loss, suicide, living with an addict, and more.

Chapter Seven

How Can You Forgive Me After What I Have Done?

FORGIVENESS IS
AN INCREDIBLE GIFT . . .

The need to forgive and to be forgiven dwells within each of our hearts. Throughout this chapter, teens share experiences in which they looked for the Lord's forgiveness in their own lives or they sought God's strength to forgive someone else. If you identify with a particular story, I hope that it touches you with insight and direction. Forgiveness is an incredible gift from God, but it is also important to make choices every day that honor God in every way.

Mrs. T

GOD TELLS US TO HONOR
THY FATHER AND THY MOTHER . . .

I fight with my mom all the time. If it's not about this, it's about that, and if it's not about that, it's about the other. People say we fight because we're alike and hearing that scares me. I had such a hard time growing up as battles between my mom and me escalated into World War III almost daily, especially when I was in high school. I knew there was no way I'd survive if someone didn't change, and in my heart I doubted it would be my mom. The saying goes that you can't teach an old dog new tricks, and I was a younger dog, so I figured I'd have to be the one to change. But me change—ha! I'm perfect, or so I thought. So to do this and to really do it right, I had to dig deep—waaaaaaaaaay deep.

God tells us to honor thy father and thy mother, and through all of those tumultuous years, I wasn't honoring my mom. I even thought she was a bit crazy. I began to pray, mostly because I didn't know what else to do, but also because a part of me knew that the only answer to the problem was in God. So I decided, or rather God helped me see, that I had to honor my mother. With honor, love is not automatic by any means; in fact, it isn't even required. But as I began to honor my mom, my love for her felt renewed. Also, honoring my mom brought me a great deal of peace, not only in the sense of "no war," but also in the sense of tranquility. I think this feeling comes from God's forgiveness. When I finally looked to Him for guidance, I realized that I needed to ask His forgiveness for disrespecting my mom. For so long I thought it would always be a war with my mom, but God taught me otherwise. Believe me, there are still days when honoring my mother is the last thing on my mind. But even then, I remember the peace that God granted me through His forgiveness, and I am able to try just a little bit harder to be the daughter He wants me to be.

TAWNIE, 19

I WAS SO BLINDED BY
THE ATTENTION PEOPLE WERE
FINALLY PAYING TO ME . . .

I was sixteen and a half. I had just finished my sophomore year of high school. It had been both a great academic year and a year of new experiences. I had passed my road test and received my driver's license. This was the greatest thing that had happened to me yet, but I never knew that having a car and gaining my independence would change my life. I had a very busy summer. I worked many hours and spent much time with my friends. At the beginning of junior year, however, my life changed. I believe that people knew me as a good kid who never got into trouble. Well, I was sick of being the angel of my class, so I made many poor decisions that year. One of these poor decisions was drinking.

I remember the first time that I drank. It was before a school dance, and at the party everyone was shocked to see me with a beer in my hand. I was so blinded by the attention people were finally paying to me that I didn't realize I was making a terrible mistake. This one incident was the catalyst to a chain reaction. People now started to notice me, and I became more popular with every beer I drank. This problem got so bad that all I could think about was drinking on the weekend. I didn't realize that I was getting into more trouble each weekend. I had become a whole other person, someone I would have hated just a few months back.

As the year progressed, my problems worsened. I decided to try marijuana. I remember how terrible it was the first time, but that didn't stop me one bit! Just like drinking got out of control, so did drugs. Time passed, and now it was senior year. I was still drinking and smoking without a clue in the world. This drastically changed, however, when my parents found pot in my room. They were devastated to say the least. I sat through countless hours of discipline, and my heart shattered when my mom said, "We will never forgive you." When I heard this, I wanted to die. At this point, the only person I could really talk to was God. He was the only one who would listen to me. I was so depressed that I didn't know what else to do but pray and ask God to help me through this most difficult time in my life. God forgave me when no one else would. I feel that I have matured now. I occasionally look back on my experiences last year and just a few months ago, and I realize I made a terrible mistake. I also think back on how God was there for me when I needed Him the most. He gives me the courage to live life the right way now and to make good decisions.

PATRICK, 17

READER/CUSTOMER CARE SURVEY

We care about your opinions! Please take a moment to fill out our online Reader Survey at **http://survey.hcibooks.com**.

As a **"THANK YOU"** you will receive a **VALUABLE INSTANT COUPON** towards future book purchases

as well as a **SPECIAL GIFT** available only online! Or, you may mail this card back to us.

(PLEASE PRINT IN ALL CAPS)

First Name		MI.	Last Name	
Address				City
State	Zip			Email

1. Gender
- ❑ Female   ❑ Male

2. Age
- ❑ 8 or younger
- ❑ 9-12   ❑ 13-16
- ❑ 17-20   ❑ 21-30
- ❑ 31+

3. Did you receive this book as a gift?
- ❑ Yes   ❑ No

4. How did you find out about the book?
- ❑ Friend
- ❑ School
- ❑ Parent

- ❑ Online
- ❑ Store Display
- ❑ Teen Magazine
- ❑ Interview/Review

5. Where do you usually buy books?
(please choose one)
- ❑ Bookstore
- ❑ Online
- ❑ Book Club/Mail Order
- ❑ Price Club (Sam's Club, Costco's, etc.)
- ❑ Retail Store (Target, Wal-Mart, etc.)

6. What magazines do you like to read? *(please choose one)*
- ❑ Teen Vogue
- ❑ Seventeen
- ❑ CosmoGirl
- ❑ Rolling Stone
- ❑ Teen Ink
- ❑ Christian Magazines
- ❑ Other

7. What books do you like to read? *(please choose one)*
- ❑ Fiction
- ❑ Self-help
- ❑ Reality Stories/Memoirs
- ❑ Sports

8. What attracts you most to a book?
(please choose one)
- ❑ Title
- ❑ Cover Design
- ❑ Author
- ❑ Content

TAPE IN MIDDLE; DO NOT STAPLE

BUSINESS REPLY MAIL

FIRST-CLASS MAIL PERMIT NO 45 DEERFIELD BEACH, FL

POSTAGE WILL BE PAID BY ADDRESSEE

Chicken Soup for the Soul®
Teens Talkin' Faith
3201 SW 15th Street
Deerfield Beach FL 33442-9875

FOLD HERE

Comments

Do you have your own Chicken Soup story
that you would like to send us?
Please submit at: **www.chickensoup.com**

Books for Life

. . . I FELT SO GUILTY . . .

I cannot tell a lie. That doesn't mean that I have never cheated or lied. I mean, I'm not perfect; I just can't live with myself after I do it. One time in sixth grade, we were taking a geography test. I didn't know the answer to a question, so I decided to look on my partner's paper. I didn't really feel like I consciously chose to do this, but it was like something took over my brain, and I cheated without even thinking about it. I wanted to get 100 percent so badly that I forced myself to do the wrong thing. In the moment, I couldn't really see the harm in it. But slowly, it started to bother me. *It was just a simple little test,* I kept telling myself to try to clear my conscience. By the time the bell rang at the end of the day, I felt so guilty I could barely function. I finally cracked and told my mom all that happened and how I felt about it. My mom was pretty disappointed in me, but she told me to do whatever I needed to do to make it right. The next day, I decided to go to my teacher and tell her the truth about what I did and how I wanted to make it better. She appreciated that I told the truth, and all the pieces just fell into place. Now it's not just this one past experience that caused my conscience to fall all over me; it happens whenever I do anything even remotely wrong, like when I really want to keep something a secret, but I can't. It's like a whole bunch of butterflies are released into my stomach right after I do a bad deed, and I can't do anything else until I tell the truth. After the whole "cheating on the test" dilemma, though, I realized that God made me who I am for a reason. It's like He's showing me which path to take in life. Sometimes I think my conscience is God's way of assisting me when I do something wrong. God wants me to always be truthful, and I really am because of the conscience He gave me.

CARLOTTA, 14

. . . WHY DID I FEEL SO ALONE?

I was raised in the church, I had a Christian family, and my mother grounded God's Word into my heart. I was so in love with Jesus . . . but sometimes you fall down, and you fall hard. Sometimes you make new friends; mine was the bottle. Sometimes you happen to change. I changed everything, and not for the better. I forgot who I was. As a Christian, yes, I knew right from wrong. But as a teenager, I didn't even care. At fourteen, I thought I was having the best year of my life. Experiencing everything for the first time was the best feeling I'd ever had, or so I thought at the time. Sneaking out gave me an adrenaline boost. Speeding through the midnight streets made my heart pound, and getting wasted at parties made my mind race. The booze kept me calm, the pills were my back-up, and my older friends were always there for me, but why did I still feel so alone?

Fighting, swearing, yelling, and loneliness became normal in my family. I wanted to escape. I tried cutting, but that didn't make me any more satisfied with life. I tried sex. I knew I wasn't ready, but I let it happen anyway. There isn't a day that goes by without my brain getting wrapped around every painful decision I made. Drowning in the reality of pain and heartache had finally begun to break me down. I knew that nothing the world could say to me would help, and I knew no one could save me. It had been six months since I had last spoken with God, but now I screamed at Him. Over and over, I walked the lonely roads in the late-night hours, asking Him where He'd been. Why was I so confused, hurt, scared, depressed, and alone? I was acting as if He was the enemy, but as I walked and screamed, I figured out that I was my own worst enemy. I was feeding on chaos and living in sin. Right then, an overwhelming feeling of peace washed over me. I didn't feel alone anymore. It was as if something or someone was guiding me home. I'd like to believe I had angels by my side, and maybe I did. Changing my life and asking for forgiveness are truly the hardest things I've ever done in my short life. I'm still in the process, but if that means an eternity in heaven someday, where I will feel peace and never be lonely, then it's worth it!

ISELLA, 14

AUTHOR'S NOTE: If you or someone you know has tried to escape life's pressures and problems through the use of drugs, sex, or cutting, please know that these options are not solutions. They only lead to more anguish and heartbreak. Please seek help. Talk to someone you trust or refer to the resources in the Appendix at the back of this book.

. . . GOD IS VERY PATIENT . . .

Most people want God to forgive them for things they regret they've done or for things they did wrong against His will or in His eyes. In my case, I want God to forgive me for the times when I've doubted Him and His choices for my life . . . for the times I thought I was right and He was wrong. God has a plan for all of us. He knows what is best for us. He's in control, and He loves us. So, I think to myself, *How could I ever doubt such a loving and forgiving God?*

If one of my friends were to doubt me, it would hurt my feelings. For example, if my best friend doubted that I could keep a secret, I would be crushed. I wonder if it hurts God's feelings when I doubt Him, too. Yet, He forgives me so easily. How does He do that? I think the answer is that God is very patient, and He wants me to believe in Him, which I definitely do!

Sometimes, though, people who believe in God have their doubts as well. I am so happy that God will still love us and forgive us when we doubt Him!

CARRA, 14

THIS IS WHEN GUILT COMES IN . . .

I've always wondered: What exactly is that little wave that goes over you when you've done something wrong? It starts in your brain and runs through your body, but mostly it dwells in your chest, near the middle, but slightly to the left. Guilt—the pain you must live with or confess. It can stay with you for a second or last a lifetime, depending on what action you choose to take in response to it.

When I was about ten, I went to a store with my brother. He was about fourteen then. I was fascinated with all the various charms they had to put on necklaces. Having this child's curiosity and no money, somehow the pretty trinkets found their way into my pocket. We left the store and went home, and I looked over my new treasures. This is when guilt comes in. You know it is wrong, but either way you go, you lose because you've already made a poor choice in the first place. I think that the feeling of guilt may be God's way of helping you to do what is right. So the story ends by my parents finding out and making me take them back and apologize. Through my parents and my conscience, God showed me the right way, and I will never steal anything again.

VALERI, 13

I'VE FOUND THE ANSWER TO ALL THEIR PROBLEMS AND TO MINE . . .

When I was a young teen, I made some poor choices. I started out smoking pot, but that led to me using other drugs. Soon, things got out of control, and it seemed that I was ruining my life. Then, something incredible happened. I quit everything—all of the drugs and other bad choices I had made. I decided to pursue a relationship— a relationship like one I have never had. It was a relationship filled with unconditional love. I'm talking about a relationship with God. Everywhere I go and everything I hear from people these days is usually about all the problems they have or things that aren't going right for them. I've found the answer to all their problems and to mine: God! That's why I realized I was going nowhere. God had bigger and better plans for me. I can't tell you how nice it is just to know that I've always got somewhere to turn. Everything isn't perfect now, but it's a hundred times better than it was before. Through God's grace, I quit doing drugs. I quit drinking. I quit smoking. One thing I am not going to quit is this race. I'm going to stay in the battle, and I am fighting on the right side—God's.

ZACHARIA, 18

AUTHOR'S NOTE: If you or someone you know is using alcohol or other drugs and would like to stop, you can call the National Referral Organization at 1-800-454-8966 for information on a treatment program near you.

I FINALLY REALIZED
THAT FORGIVENESS IS SOMETHING
TO CHERISH . . .

I started going to church when my mom married my stepdad, and at the beginning I was unsure and felt out of place. But soon I became a Christian, and church and all that it entailed became a way of life. But not long after I was baptized, I began to feel like I was taking advantage of my religion. After I was told that God forgives you no matter what, I found myself doing things that I wouldn't normally do, only because I knew at the time that I would be forgiven for it afterward.

Someone once told me that you have a jar inside your soul for all of your sins. If that is true, then the jar in my soul was overflowing. Something in my heart just clicked, and I knew that I was doing the wrong thing. Now, I think hard before I do anything because I know that there will be consequences for my actions, even if I sincerely ask God to forgive me. I finally realized that forgiveness is something to cherish and not to take for granted.

CHERISE, 14

I KNOW THAT GOD FORGIVES ME . . .

God blessed me with a learning disability. Now, most people would say that a learning disability isn't a blessing, but I think it is. It is what makes me special. I didn't always feel that way, though. For a long time, I was mad at God because of my disability. It was hardest for me when I was in class, and the teacher would ask me to read out loud. I would just ask God why He had to give it to me. Eventually, I learned that I shouldn't be mad at God because I have become such a stronger person because of my learning struggles. I know that God forgives me for being angry at Him. I also know that He gave this to me for a reason, and I accept it now, just like God accepts me!

REBECCA, 14

. . . I ENDED UP BEING ALMOST A SHADOW OF HER . . .

For many teenagers, the thought of high school is both exhilarating and nervewracking. The first weeks are filled with new classes and teachers, new friends and experiences. The excitement of a fresh year is often quickly replaced by the struggle to fit in and be accepted. In the beginning of my freshman year, my innocence to the ways of high school showed through in all of my thoughts and actions. I had never experienced the typical "girl drama," and up until that year, boys had always been more my friends than anything else. I had grown up in a Christian home and had a fairly strong relationship with God. My friends and family were the core of my life, and I never expected that to change. However, it did when I met Amanda.

Amanda was the type of girl almost everybody liked. She was bouncy, cute, and funny, and she knew how to get people to want to be around her. Yet, underneath Amanda's seemingly attractive personality, there was a whole other side that most people didn't see. From the beginning of the school year, I was drawn to Amanda. I appreciated her friendship and did everything I could to keep us in agreement. But after about a month, I began to question some of the things she did and said. I often heard her make rude comments about people in our classes or in the halls. She even said things about kids she didn't even know, including some upperclassmen. After hearing some of the things she said about others, I realized that I would do whatever it took to keep her from viewing me like that. Consequently, I ended up being almost a shadow of her. I abandoned my childhood friends for her, simply because in her eyes they "weren't good enough." I lost all contact with God because my focus was always on my friendship with Amanda. My true friends never wanted to be around me anymore, and I was constantly in conflict with my family. Gone was my little-girl innocence. I had become someone I couldn't even relate to. Letting Amanda have so much of an influence over me slowly began to wear away at who I really was, creating a person I never wanted to know or be.

Eventually, even Amanda abandoned me. We had a single argument, and the foundation that our friendship was on crumbled. I became the target of her slurs and quickly found myself alone and without a single friend to depend on. I expected that everyone had given up on me, even God. But God has a way of drawing a broken soul back to Him. It took me a while to figure out that the person I had become was not who God intended me to be. I realized that in all of my confusion, God had always been there, patiently waiting for me to come back to Him. I remember going to bed one night and just praying for mercy and forgiveness. I apologized for turning away from Him, along with my friends and family. I confessed how much I needed God's guidance in my life to get me through the day.

A year later, I am still regretting some of my lost friendships. But mostly I regret losing my friendship with God during that time in my life. While I am on the mend, I know that I still have a way to go. But now, I am headed in the right direction, with real friends, real family, and a single, real God to guide me along the way. Never lose faith in the one God you can always count on, for He's never lost faith in you.

BROOKE, 15

I PARTIED ALL THE TIME . . .

I was always searching for happiness but could never find it anywhere. Then I started to use drugs and drink. I thought, *Hey, this is what it is all about. This is what I've been looking for.* I really believed that happiness could be found with drinking and drugs. I partied all the time, and so did most of my friends. I got mixed up with the wrong group of people. I am a smart person and always did well in school, but all of a sudden all I could do was look at a blank page and know it was due the next day and I had five more to write after the first one. That's what partying did to me. Nothing was more important. I began to think that there was always time for school, but partying was in the here and now. I barely got by.

Things just kept getting harder. People started to move on and get over the party scene, but I couldn't seem to. Then somebody took me to a Bible study. I started to build a relationship with God, and I stopped using. Life started again! I could actually remember what I did two days previously and who I was calling on the telephone. God did something for me that the drinking and drugs didn't do. He gave me that peace I was always looking for. I always thought I was happy before and had real friends, but once I stopped partying, I really found out who my friends were. I know now that I will always have somebody to turn to. Even though I can't see God, I know that He is listening to everything I say. I wasted five years of my life partying. Now, I feel like I can still be somebody and go somewhere, but I know I can't do it alone.

JORGE, 19

AUTHOR'S NOTE: If you'd like to seek help for a drug or alcohol problem, I encourage you to call 1-800-454-8966 for a referral for treatment.

"T" TALK

The story that I am about to share with you is very serious and exceptionally sad. But I have chosen to share it because I believe that within this powerful story, a valuable lesson can be learned.

Courtney was only fourteen and extremely drunk on the summer night that she was raped. Her rapist was someone she considered a friend. She trusted him, and he betrayed that trust. Sadly, Courtney feels that she betrayed herself, as well. She knows that the rape was not her fault, but she blames herself for choosing to get drunk. In fact, Courtney was so drunk that when this guy, who was nineteen, asked her to come back to his room so he could show her something, she went with him, trailing her hands along the wall to maintain her balance. Once there, she began to feel sick. He told her to lie down on his bed and that he would stay with her and protect her. Apparently, Courtney passed out. The next thing she remembered, she felt like she was being shaken. It was only then that she realized she was being forced to have sex. Courtney struggled as she screamed, hoping that her friends down the hall would hear her. She pleaded and begged him to stop. Finally, he did, saying, "I was finished with you anyway." When he walked away, he took Courtney's virginity with him.

Courtney cried as she told me her story. She felt worthless, dirty, and guilty. "How could somebody do that?" she asked. But she also wondered how she could let herself get into that situation? Courtney kept the rape a secret for almost two months, as her dignity and self-confidence disintegrated. Finally, no longer able to hide from the truth, Courtney confessed the rape to her parents and the authorities so that it would not go unpunished.

Still, Courtney carried a heavy burden on her shoulders. She felt an intense emptiness inside and began to shut out everyone. Even her mom, who was there for Courtney in every way, could not fill the void that was growing in her heart. Her mom told her, "It's going to be okay, Court. I'm here for you." But Courtney didn't feel it would be okay. She didn't understand how she could ever overcome her feelings of hopelessness. Many people, myself included, pleaded with Courtney not to blame herself. I specifically told Courtney that it is never the fault of the victim for being raped. If a person does not give consent, resists, or says "no" and is forced to have sex, it is rape, and only the assailant can take the blame. Yet, when she thought about the party scene that she had become involved in over the summer, she was afraid she had disappointed God.

Courtney remembers a particular night when she threw herself across her bed, sobbing and pleading with God. Tears streaked her face as she prayed, "God, please don't let me wake up in the morning." Immediately, she felt at peace—not because she thought God would grant her prayer, but because she knew the opposite was occurring. Courtney said that as she lay on her bed, she sensed God's presence. She felt as if He physically wrapped His arms around her, and she began to feel whole again. Courtney experienced an unwavering conviction that she was still accepted by God, and that with His forgiveness and help she would get through her ordeal.

God's grace is abundant. His mercy abounds. Teens often assume that God will turn His back on them if they make a poor choice or do something they regret. Maybe they think this way because they have experienced this type of reaction from their friends. It is not uncommon for friends to, at least temporarily, turn against each other if they have been hurt or disappointed. For example, if a close friend betrays your confidence, even after you make up, you may harbor hurt or anger toward that person. Although you love your friend, there may be a small part of you that can never forgive his or her disloyalty. Fortunately, God's love is much bigger than our love. When God forgives you, He forgives forever. He never brings it back and throws it in your face. When He forgives, He is able to forget, too.

My friend Janell uses a fantastic analogy to demonstrate God's grace and forgiveness. She tells the story of an experience she encountered at a Christian retreat. She awoke early one morning and decided she needed some quiet time. With a cup of tea in hand, she walked down to a river. As she stood by the river, she began to contemplate all of the wonderful Christians at this retreat. Compared to them, she felt unworthy. As she prayed, she pondered the mistakes she had made in her life, all of her failures and sins, and she found herself staring down at her cup of tea. Brown in color, the tea looked dirty and stagnant. Janell felt much the same way. Then she looked at the river. It was running gloriously clear, clean, and beautiful. In what she believes was an answer to prayer, Janell felt God encouraging her to throw her tea into the river. It was as if He was saying, "Give me your worries and your troubles. Give me your regrets and faults, and I will sweep them away in this river. Never will they come back. Your life can flow clear and clean now, no longer dirty or stagnant." As Janell emptied the contents of her cup into the river, she noticed that her tea didn't taint the beautiful rushing water and, in that moment, she felt refreshed, renewed, and worthy.

Like Janell, there may be times in your life when you feel undeserving of God's love. Teenagers frequently make choices they later regret. Sometimes it is difficult for teens to think beyond the moment. When you're at a party and every-one is drinking and seeming to have fun, it is easy to rational-ize drinking yourself. But when I speak to youth groups, I always tell teens that drinking and God don't mix. Not only does God use the Bible to tell us that drunkenness is a sin, but think about it: When you drink, you lose your ability to make sound decisions. Even if you set limits for your drinking, those boundaries are often broken. It is more common for one drink to turn into five than for a teen to stop at just one.

Many teens who choose to use drugs or have sex for the first time do so after they have been drinking. I have spoken with teenagers who regret having lost their virginity after a night of partying. They want to take it back, but they can't. They are worried about sexually transmitted diseases and pregnancy. But they hadn't thought about it at the time because under the influence of alcohol, they had lost their sense of good judgment. Rape, too, is a risk. Courtney said that had she been thinking clearly, she wouldn't have gone alone into a bedroom with a guy who was five years older than her. Nor would she have passed out, leaving him the opportunity to violate her.

Also, the use of drugs and alcohol among teens is not only illegal with consequences of arrest but teenagers who drink and use also risk their lives. Many studies indicate that the leading cause of teen death is accidents, and the majority of these are related to substance abuse. Remember Brandy's story at the beginning of this book? Finally, teens who choose to use drugs or alcohol jeopardize their freedom. I'm not referring to jail time, although that can be a realistic result. I am talking about addiction.

If you use drugs or alcohol habitually, you risk addiction and can become a prisoner of your need. Scripture teaches that your physical body is the temple of the Holy Spirit. How can you serve God and addiction, too?

It is also important to understand that when considering your physical body as the temple of the Holy Spirit, in addition to abstaining from drugs and alcohol, it is spiritually right to be abstinent from sex before marriage. I have read several references to a study that indicated half of all teens surveyed were sexually active or had been at some point in their teen years. That tells me two things. First, if you are a virgin, praise God! Know that you are not alone—50 percent of your peers value their virginity, too. Second, there are teenagers out there who are making a choice to be sexually active. But I already knew this from speaking with my students or kids in youth groups. The choice for teens to be sexually active can be a matter of curiosity, acceptance, or temptation. Yet, regardless of a person's reason, the Bible has something to say about it.

God speaks often in the Bible of sexual immorality as a sin. Also, God calls us to save ourselves for the person we marry. The Bible tells us to refrain from sex until marriage because sexual intercourse is a sacred and intimate act that should only be shared within the union of husband and wife. Within the sanctity of marriage, sexual intimacy can be a wonderful experience and a blessing. God didn't say, "Sex is bad!" In fact, He created sex. Don't forget, though, He also gave us boundaries for sexual behavior. I encourage you to save sex for marriage. Offer it to your husband or wife on your wedding night as a precious gift that you have treasured and withheld to share with the person with whom you want to spend the rest of your life.

I have had many teens ask me, "How can I rate with God after what I've done?" Regardless of the choice that a teen may have made to lead to his or her need for forgiveness, God lays out the answer for us plainly. The Bible proclaims that if we feel sorry for what we have done and we sincerely ask God to forgive us, He will. God lifts the burden of sin from our hearts and grants us His mercy. Like the free-flowing river, God doesn't recycle past sins. When He forgives, He forgives forever, and His grace overflows.

Mrs. T

AUTHOR'S NOTE: I realize that Courtney's story is very tragic, and I pray that you never experience such an ordeal. However, I feel compelled to give you the following information as a resource: Rape, Abuse and Incest National Network (RAINN), 1-800-656-4673.

Chapter Eight

Hey, God, Can You Hear Me Way Up There?

... *PRAYER CAN ACTUALLY BRING YOU TO GOD* ...

I chose this chapter title because I know that some teens feel as if God is "too far away" to actually talk to. However, when you read passages from this chapter, I believe that you will see how close prayer can actually bring you to God. Teens share their stories and their philosophies of prayer. I pray that you will take from their testimonies a notion of the peace, comfort, strength, and hope that can be found in having a conversation with the Lord.

Mrs. T

I TELL GOD ABOUT
MY PLANS . . .

I have not been to church in over four years. Every Sunday, I selfishly sleep in until the sun is so bright that I can sleep no longer. I do, however, pray every day. At night, when I have gotten off the phone from talking to my friends or my boyfriend, I turn off all the lights, get into bed, and have a nice talk with God. I tell God all about my day, what I enjoyed, and what upset me. I tell God about my plans for the next day, and that I hope He protects me while I sleep. I always thank God for giving me such wonderful people in my life. I thank Him for allowing me to be a healthy, happy, intelligent sixteen-year-old girl whose biggest worry is what I am going to wear the next day or if I did all of my homework. I like to pray for all the people in the world who are scared, sick, cold, hungry, or hurting in any way.

Talking to God each night makes me feel incredibly blessed and lucky for the life the Lord has given me. When I take time to reflect on my day by talking to God, it makes me happy to be alive. The Lord makes my daily problems and frustrations feel very insignificant compared to the love He has shown me. Since I was very young, I have seen God as an open journal. Each night I record my feelings and thoughts. He reads them over and guides me on what to do. God is always listening. God is your oldest and best friend. He knows everything about you and does not judge you. Talking to God every day is very good for letting go of stress. It helps me to relax and feel at peace. I fall asleep knowing that I am loved by Him and that all of His children are here for a reason. Never be afraid to tell God anything. He already knows what you are going to say. The Lord is a patient friend when you feel you have no one.

KINZIE, 16

. . . MY BROTHER DROWNED IN THE BATHTUB . . .

God answers prayers in countless different ways—some you would expect and some you have no idea are coming. When I was very young, God answered my family's prayers with something we never would have thought or wanted, but we can see the blessing in it today.

When I was around three years old, my parents went on vacation and left my fourteen-month-old brother and me with the babysitter. One day, the babysitter left my brother and me in the bathtub while she was cooking grilled-cheese sandwiches. In a moment that changed our lives forever, my brother drowned in the bathtub, and the babysitter was unable to do anything about it. I had no idea what was going on because I was too young, and all I remember are the paramedics putting these black things on my brother's chest. It took awhile to reach my parents, but when we did, we were all praying for a miracle. We prayed and prayed, but God did not answer our prayers the way we thought he might.

The doctor approached my parents and said that Colby, my brother, was not going to make it. He asked if we would like to donate his organs. My parents had not even considered this question before, but they decided to say "yes." This small word worked great miracles in the lives of other people. Colby's kidneys saved a man around twenty years old from dying. His liver saved a young girl, and his heart went to a young boy and saved his life. The young boy and his family are now great friends with our family, and we try to visit each other every year. It is such a wonderful feeling to know that Colby still lives on in those three other people and that he made other people's prayers come true. Our prayers were answered, too, just not in the way we wanted them to be. This just goes to show that even if God doesn't help you exactly like you think He should, He is always listening and working in our lives. If you look in the right places, you will find Him.

T. J., 17

I KNEW AT THAT MOMENT
GOD WAS TRYING TO TELL
ME SOMETHING . . .

I have learned that God is so incredibly amazing that words can't even describe it. It took quite an act from God for me to learn this lesson, though. When I was younger, I would pray, read the Bible, go to church, and try to act in the "WWJD" way, but then, for whatever reason, it all started to fade. I felt like God wasn't there anymore. All my efforts to be a good person appeared to be useless. Yeah, Jesus died on the cross, but so what? Why should I have to honor that? I used to, but the thought of how great He was slipped quickly from my head and my heart. I was at church one Sunday and said to myself, *Why am I here?* I got up, went outside, sat on the ground, and said, "God, if you're really there, show Yourself to me." He knew I felt left out and alone, and that at that moment I needed Him more than ever.

He revealed Himself to me, not once, but twice that day. The first time, I was sitting at a table with a group of friends after church, and a guy happened to be reading his

Bible at that same table. I glanced over to check out what he was reading. It was Psalm 27. I didn't think much of it and continued my conversation. About two hours later, I couldn't believe what I saw. A man walked by me, and right across the front of his shirt it said: Psalm 27. I knew at that moment God was trying to tell me something, and I had to read Psalm 27! I went home, opened my Bible, and read, "Hear my voice when I call, O Lord; be merciful to me and answer me." This was from verse 7. Verse 9 went on to say, "Do not hide your face from me, do not turn your servant away in anger; you have been my helper. Do not reject me or forsake me, O God my Savior." Those two verses and that whole entire Psalm changed my life for- ever. The fact that God cannot only hear us when we pray but also understand us is so amazing. So, is Jesus real? ABSOLUTELY! All ya' gotta do is pray!

KYLE, 15

WHEN I PRAY,
I START OFF BY . . .

When life isn't going so great, I have a strong urge to talk to Jesus. I stop what I am doing and get down to praying. I pray because Jesus is the most important thing in my life, and just knowing that He died for my sins and is always with me makes me want to pray to Him. When I pray, I start off by admitting that I am a sinner. I ask Him to forgive me for what I have done. I tell Him that I am blessed that He is there to forgive me. I tell Him that I love Him, and that His love and glory will never leave my soul. I trust in Him, and I know that He will never abandon me. When I am done pouring my heart out to God, I tell Him what's on my mind, I sing praises to Him, or I just let Him know that I am happy that He is in my life. Praying is such a large part of my life. My spirit is lifted when I pray. The Lord has blessed me in so many ways that I feel guilty about all the sins I have committed. Although God lifts this guilt from my heart when He forgives me, I still pray that I will make better decisions in the future.

CALLIE, 14

I MAKE UP MY OWN
PRAYERS . . .

You know that "easy button" from that commercial on TV? Well, for me praying to God is like having my own easy button. No, I don't instantly get my every wish granted, but I have someone to talk to who is easy to contact and always available. Praying to God is easy because I know that He's there and will listen. Even though there is only one way to push the easy button, there are many ways to pray to God. You can pray spontaneously, when you feel the urge to talk to someone. You can pray before or after you eat, when you want to show God appreciation for the delicious meal and for the person who prepared it. You can pray when you wake up and those rays of sunlight are trickling through your window, and you just want to shout for joy at the beauty of it. And you can pray after you have a long day and you need to let out all the anger or sorrow that built up at school or while doing something else.

For me, I like to pray when I feel the need all of a sudden. It may be because I've got a big game. Just being able to talk to someone who won't tell me what I did wrong if I lose or play badly gives me the strength to keep going even when I feel tired and frustrated. Or maybe when I walk outside and the stars are perfect and the air has a touch of breeze that wraps around me, it makes me want to thank whoever is responsible. I make up my own prayers and say whatever might be on my mind. The best part is that when I talk to God, I can do it without feeling judged and without worrying about sounding stupid or getting embarrassed. I believe that everyone who prays also has prayers that seem to go unanswered. I think the reason is because God probably knows what's good for us, more than we do. God knows what our life should be like, and He has a bigger plan that we are a part of, if we choose to accept His will for us. That's right, God has a will for each of us, but He gave us free choice. If you choose to, you can skip out on His big plan for you. Or you can pray and follow Him. It's as "easy" as that!

AUDREY, 14

I FEEL I CAN SAY
ANYTHING TO HIM . . .

I pray to God because I feel when I talk to Him, He truly listens. I feel I can say anything to Him, and He will understand. I pray to God because some things I am just not comfortable saying in front of others. So I say them to God because I know that He is always listening and will always understand what I am going through.

NATHAN, 14

I'VE LIVED WITH MY GRANDPARENTS FOR TEN YEARS . . .

I never used to pray for help from God as much as I should have, but since this recent court case with my mom and dad, I've learned to pray as much as I can.

I've lived with my grandparents for ten years, and I feel like they're my parents now. My mom and dad want to take that away from me, and they don't understand how I feel or what I want. They only care about themselves. I started to live with my grandparents in the first place because my mom and dad weren't married, they were both drug users, and my dad was violent and beat my mom and all of his other girlfriends. My mom and I had to go to a battered women's shelter. My grandma offered to take me for a while until my mom got her stuff together. My mom agreed, and a little while turned into seven years. During this time, my grandparents got custody of me. I was glad because I didn't want to go back to my mom or dad.

A little while after I turned twelve, my mom and dad took me and my grandparents to court. Before the day of court, I prayed my heart out that I could stay with my grandparents. I knew that my grandparents and I would need God's courage to get through this battle, so I prayed for that, too. The day of court, my mom and dad both lied. They said they weren't on drugs, which they were, and my dad said he wasn't violent. My mom also said that my grandparents stole me from her, which was completely untrue. So after court, I prayed that everything was going to be all right.

Now, I know that sometimes when you pray, it doesn't always work out like you want, but when we went back to court to hear the judge's decision, I was amazed that we got what we wanted and more. My mom and dad made some bad choices, and it finally caught up with them. The judge saw through it, and so did I. Right now, I love my mom and dad, but I will never live with them or be as close to them as I am with my real parents—my grandma and grandpa!

LAUREN, 12

AUTHOR'S NOTE: If you are able to identify with Lauren's situation because you live in the presence of addiction and/or abuse, please seek help. The following resources can lead you to support services in your area: National Youth Crisis Hotline: 1-800-HIT-HOME (1-800-448-4663); National Resource Center on Domestic Violence: 1-800-537-2238.

Do I ever worry about being late for God?

"Mom, will you turn on the light so I can see the dark?" I asked this question of my mom when I was three years old. I was riding in my car seat while my mom was driving at night. Over the years, my mom has told me this story many times, as my question continues to remind her to shine the light of God onto the darker things in life. What are some darker things in life? For me, not trusting God with my problems keeps me in the dark. Nothing will ever be done about my problems without God's help. Whenever I have problems, I go to my room and pray, giving all my troubles to God. Also, I know that God is always there, but sometimes I am not there for God. Being too busy for God is another way I end up in the dark. How many times have I thought, *I'm going to be late for soccer!* Do I ever worry about being late for God? Sometimes it feels like it's hard to have God on my mind, especially if I have activities outside of school like I do when I play soccer. I am learning to take God with me at all times wherever I go. I am also learning that I need to appreciate God by praying to Him and thanking Him every day. Now when

I pray, I often ask the same question I asked when I was three years old. Instead of asking my mom, though, I ask God the question: "God, will You turn on the light so I can see the dark?" I know God's brilliant love will shine on me forever and transform my dark into light.

JOSEPH, 14

DOES HE STILL LISTEN TO MY PRAYERS?

I often think, *Is God still protecting my soul? Does He still listen to my prayers? Does He still feel my pain? Or, does He look down on me for the choices I have made in my life?* When I pray at night, I let God know that I am sorry for the sins I have committed, but there is nothing I or God can do to change those decisions. If someone were to ask me if I am ashamed of ever doing drugs, I would say "no" because now that I am off drugs, I feel that I am stronger in a way.

There is no way to change the bad decisions we make in life, but we can learn from our mistakes and make better choices in the future. By doing this, it makes us stronger. So, do I think God still listens to my prayers or shares my pain? Yes, I do, because I feel that no matter what kind of choices I make, God is still with me to help me and to show me a better way. God won't make us do the right thing. All He can do is show us the path to follow. It is our choice to actually follow that path.

CURT, 16

I PRAY WHEN I AM
ON THE GO . . .

I pray for two reasons: to ask God for something, and to thank Him. He is all-powerful. I pray when I am on the go. I'll have something to pray about, and I'll stop for a minute and think of God. I may petition, or I may thank Him. But then I am back on my way feeling that God is with me. In asking for something, I never try to test God. I trust that He is all-knowing and that the answer to my prayer is the answer I need. So I pray open-minded prayers. My favorite prayer, the one most meaningful to me, is, "God, Thy will be done." It reminds me that God is in control, so whatever happens is His will, out of His goodness, grace, and understanding. And sometimes things don't go exactly as I would like them to, but I know that though I may not understand why, God does, and I have to trust His answers.

PHILLIP, 17

. . . GOD IS THERE TO TALK TO ALWAYS . . .

When I was a lttle girl, I used to pray every night before I went to bed. It was something I was taught to do. Mom said there was something about having your hands in such a position that would reach God so He could know you had something to say to Him. As I grew up, my prayers changed. They slowly grew to mean more and more. But then I stopped praying for a while, until about five months ago. That is when I found out that my grandma had cancer, and since then I've never prayed so much in my life.

When I first found out, flashes of memory came back to me of when I was ten and my grandpa died of cancer. I knew what was next for my grandma, and I didn't like it. My grandpa's death was the hardest thing I've ever had to deal with since I've been alive. After Grandpa died of cancer, my routine praying stopped. In fact, I rarely ever prayed. I know it's wrong, but I got so mad at God for taking someone so special from me, especially after all the times I prayed to Him, asking Him not to take my grandpa away from me. I figured God must not be listening to me in my prayers. I had no desire to talk to God after that . . . until I heard about Grandma.

Once I found out that Grandma had cancer and only a 50 percent chance of it being removed, I realized there was no way that I could get through this alone. I needed help. My grandma is one of the most important people in my life. When my mom got off the phone and told me through thick tears that Grandma had cancer, I exploded. I remember punching my fists into the walls and screaming, "No!" All thoughts of my grandpa dying of cancer raced through my mind. This couldn't happen to Grandma, too. How could God do this? I had to ask Him. The only way I was taught to talk to God was through recited prayers. The difference now was I found myself always praying for my grandma, with any words I could find in my heart. I would pray while I was on the phone, in class, during my softball games, everywhere. I also found that you don't have to fold your hands to reach up and talk to God. In fact, you don't even have to move your lips. I prayed all of the time.

Grandma went into surgery, and a few days later, the results of the procedure were given to us. When I heard the cancer had been completely removed, I cried almost as hard as I did when I found out she had it. I was so relieved, and the hurt inside started to leave me. It's such a great feeling. I thank God for this because I know He had everything to do with it. I know now, looking back on those days when I didn't pray, that it wasn't right for me to be angry at Him. My grandpa is gone now, and that is something I have to live with every day of my life. But I know now that everything happens for a reason. Even though God didn't make my grandparents have cancer, I learned from both situations. I also know now that God is there to talk to always. Even if it seems like He's not listening, He is. He listens to everyone.

SABRINA, 14

. . . THE COPS CAME AND BUSTED EVERYONE . . .

I pray several times a day. I always have. I don't exactly know why, but it comforts me when I talk to God because I know He's always listening. He knows what is best for me, so I have to trust that He'll make the right decision for me. I remember a little while ago there was a party that I really wanted to be invited to. I prayed and prayed for God to let me be invited, but I wasn't. I was angry for a while—even a little at God because I felt like He didn't answer my prayer. The day after the party, I heard that drugs and alcohol were being used there all night long. And whether they wanted to or not, everyone had taken part in some way. Later that night at the party, the cops came and busted everyone. A few people were even taken to juvenile hall. Then I realized that God hadn't answered my prayer for a reason. He protected me. And now I know that no matter how much I may disagree, He'll always make the best decisions for me because He loves me.

MICHAELA, 14

. . . WHEN I FEEL LIKE LIFE IS WEIGHING ME DOWN, I PRAY . . .

"If you just can't take it, take it to the Lord." That would make a great magnet. Although it may seem cheesy, it's true. Sometimes when I feel like life is weighing me down, I pray. I take it to the Lord. To me, prayer is just like talking to my father. You don't need to be anyone special to talk to God. In fact, He wants you to talk to Him. When I pray, I feel like a burden has been lifted from my shoulders.

One of the many prayers God has answered for me is when He delivered my mom from drugs. She wasn't into them heavily, but just enough to break our family apart. Ever since I could remember, my parents would be fighting, or my mom would move out for a while and stay with her friends. When this would happen, my dad, whom I admire very much, wouldn't get all worked up and yell; he would pray. As a matter of fact, I can remember an instance when we were standing in the kitchen, and my dad held my hands. We prayed that my mom would realize sooner rather than later that she couldn't live without

God in her life. That was seven years ago, and we are only now beginning to see the benefit of our prayers. So, when you talk to God, you need to be patient. Results don't often happen overnight. And even when prayers are answered, we still need to pray to God and thank Him for everything.

OLIVIA, 14

AUTHOR'S NOTE: If someone in your family has a problem with addiction, I encourage you to call Al-Anon/Alateen at 1-800-356-9996. They can refer you to support services for family members of addicts.

"T" TALK

My friend Laura's mom had been in the hospital's intensive care unit for three weeks, battling complications from uterine cancer. She had drifted into a coma and depended on a respirator to breathe. She was bleeding internally, and her blood pressure had dropped so low that the doctors had called the family together to prepare them for the inevitable. They told Laura, along with her father and two brothers, that they didn't expect her mother to make it through the night. If the family wanted to say good-bye, they'd better do it quickly. At that point, there was no hope for recovery. Laura and her family went directly to her mom's room. Laura remembers telling her mother, "Mom, if you want to fight to live, now is the time. You have to do it now!" Yet, on the way home to get blankets and pillows to take back to the hospital so that they could stay by her mom's side on what would surely be her last night, Laura's conviction that her mom could fight to live deteriorated into hopelessness and desperation.

Once home, Laura left her dad sobbing on the couch while she went upstairs to gather bedding. On the way upstairs, she took a book full of prayers and scripture verses from the bookshelf. She entered her bedroom and then crumbled to the floor as desperate tears poured from her eyes. Feeling distraught and alone, she prayed to God. "This is all happening too fast," she told Him. "You haven't answered one of my prayers. God, have You abandoned me? Where are You?" And then Laura said that as she lay on the floor, hysterically sobbing, she begged God, "Lord, please give me something. If You are going to take my mother, give me something to let me know that You are real, that You can hear me. Give me something that will bring me comfort in this pain."

At that point, Laura opened her book to a random page, and the words leapt off the paper and filled her heart with peace. For they said, "Believe in Me and do not doubt, for I am here. I am with you. Trust me." Laura said that the instant she read those words, she knew deep inside her heart that not only had God given her comfort but He also answered her prayer with a feeling of absolute assurance that her mom would be okay. She said that all the fear and hopelessness she had felt when she came upstairs extraordinarily vanished into an overwhelming sense of calm. In fact, Laura said she felt bathed in peace.

Laura went directly downstairs and hugged her heartbroken father. "Dad," she said, "Mom will be okay." Laura's brothers pulled her aside and asked her not to make this harder on their father. They were sure that Laura's hope was desperate and futile. But Laura didn't let them discourage her. The Holy Spirit had touched her heart. God had answered her prayer. Laura believed like she had never believed before.

They had only been gone an hour when they arrived back at the hospital. Laura's dad had stopped to talk with someone in the lobby, while Laura went to her mom's room. Miraculously, but of no surprise to Laura, her mother's blood pressure was up, her need for extra oxygen was down, and her condition was stabilizing. Laura ran down the hall to tell her father. She exclaimed, "Dad, you are not going to believe this!" In fact, he didn't. Knowing that he had to prepare his daughter, he told her that he knew she felt hopeful, but they still had to anticipate the unavoidable fact that her mother would die. But Laura knew that her mom would live. And she did! In the days to follow, they were able to take her mom off the respirator as she came out of her coma and began to breathe on her own. The first time that Laura's mom spoke after they removed the respirator, she confided, "I saw God's face the whole time I was asleep."

Prayer is an awesome concept. Can we really talk to God? Does He actually listen? Can He truly answer? I know that many teens, as well as adults, struggle with the immensity of prayer. But I believe that the answer to all of these questions is a resounding "Yes!" We can talk to God. He does hear because He cares about each and every one of us. And He does answer our prayers. However, I didn't always feel so confident about prayer.

I actually used to believe that you had to be especially worthy for prayer to really work. I even remember listening to the leaders of my high-school youth group pray out loud and thinking, I'll never be able to pray that well. I thought that my prayers had to be as eloquent and organized as theirs were. What I later learned, though, was that as long as your prayer is sincere, how a person prays doesn't matter to God. Well-articulated prayers are not on God's priority list. God cares what your heart is saying, not your lips.

I have spoken with many teens who say that the reason they don't pray is because they don't know how. Well, if you know how to carry on a conversation with a friend, then you can pray to God. Talk to Him. Tell Him about your day. Share with Him your worries. If you are feeling bad about something, admit that to Him, too. It will make you feel so much better inside, just to know that God knows you're sorry for what you have done. It will also allow Him an opportunity to grant you forgiveness. The Lord wants this type of relationship with you. He wants you to feel comfortable talking to Him. God also wants to answer your prayers.

It is true that some people hear God actually speak to them, but most do not. Usually, God speaks to us subtly. Sometimes, He gives us a feeling. Often, God uses self-reflection as a means to answer prayer. When we listen to our own conscience, God provides endless and steadfast responses to our prayers. Other times, He presents us with a circumstance or situation that guides our path. However, it is up to us to recognize His guidance and acknowledge His answers. Sometimes I think that God puts an answer right in front of our noses, but because it is not exactly what we expected or specifically what we asked for, we don't recognize it.

This reminds me of a story I once heard about a man who was standing on the roof of his house during a flood. The water was rising higher and moving faster. In fact, it was almost up to the edge of the roof. The man prayed to God and asked Him to rescue him. A few moments later, a couple in a small rowboat came by. They said to the man, "Get in. We will take you to safety." The man said, "Don't worry about me; God will save me." The water got even higher, and a larger rescue boat came to save the man. He sent them away, telling them that he was counting on God to rescue him. Soon, the man felt water swirling around his ankles. It moved quickly up his legs to his waist. A helicopter appeared, and rescuers begged the man to grab the rope they threw down to him. The man, with much conviction in his voice, yelled up to the chopper, "No, go save someone else. I prayed to God. I know that He will save me!" Moments later, the man was washed away by the water and drowned in the flood. When he got to heaven, he asked God, "Lord, why didn't you answer my prayer and rescue me?" God looked at the man with a wry grin on His face and said, "I did! I sent you a rowboat, a rescue boat, and a helicopter!"

You see, the man didn't recognize God's answer because he was blinded by his own expectations. Having faith that God will answer our prayers doesn't mean slacking off and just waiting for God to provide. Sometimes, I think that prayer, or even God for that matter, can be used as an excuse. For example, if you pray to God for a good after-school job, and then every day you go home after school, eat ice cream, and watch TV while you wait for God to drop a job in your lap, it just isn't going to happen. I actually believe that God expects more from us than that. He gave each of us talents and abilities. He encourages us to take initiative. His answers aren't always obvious or immediate. Sometimes we learn lessons while we wait. That, in itself, is a gift from God.

At the same time, occasionally His answer occurs in an

unanswered prayer. For example, you may pray with intensity about getting together with a particular guy or girl whom you have been in love with forever. Yet, your prayer may go unanswered. This doesn't happen because God wants to see you sad or deprived. It is more likely that He knows this person isn't right for you. God can see a bigger picture than we can. He can see what lies ahead of us, while we are limited by our needs of the moment. This may also explain why miracles sometimes occur, while other times they don't. My friend Laura's answered prayer was an obvious miracle. However, I know many people who have prayed intensely for a miracle, yet nothing happens. Sometimes we just have to trust that God knows what is best for us. Likely, what appears to be an unanswered prayer to us is actually answered as "wait" or "no" from God.

Perhaps you are reading this, and you've never prayed before. You can start by letting your first prayer be one that establishes a relationship with God. Ask Him to enter your heart and fill you with His Spirit. He wants that more than anything. I was speaking with a girl once who told me that it made her uncomfortable to pray. The more we talked about it, the more she realized that although she was trying to talk to God, she didn't have a personal relationship with Him. It would be like trying to start up an intimate conversation with a stranger in an elevator. You will be hindered by the boundaries of your remoteness.

Yet if you open your heart to the Lord, I think you'll find that He is pretty easy to talk to. You will also discover that prayer is very rewarding. Sharing our worries and fears with God, as well as our triumphs and praises, is like confiding in a best friend. As Kinzie suggests in her excerpt, God is the one person that she tells everything to because He is always listening and understanding, for He knows her heart like no one else. Kinzie also knows that the answers to her life problems often reside within the power of God's love. My friend Laura learned this, too.

Laura's mom has been in remission for more than five years. Laura has told me that the spiritual experience she encountered on the eve of her mother's recovery has taught her so much. Mostly, she realized that sometimes you have to let your whole being and soul be laid down before God. Prior to her prayer of desperation, Laura had put conditions on her prayers. She had tried to stay in control, and she told God what she thought should happen, rather than surrendering her problems to Him. She said that she would pray often, but she never turned her mother's sickness and situation completely over to God. Laura would give the Lord her worries, but then quickly grab them back and let them gnaw at her heart, while they grew bigger and bigger. Now, she prays for the presence of mind and heart to truly let go and completely submit her concerns to God.

Laura also learned that answered prayers come in many forms. God touched Laura's heart and gave her reassurance in an overwhelming feeling of peace. He also guided her to the faithful words in her book that gave her the comfort and hope she had been lacking. Let Laura's lessons be guidance for you as well. Know that God gave us prayer as a means to communicate with Him. Prayer is His gift to you. Make use of it, and feel the power of God's love and guidance work in your life.

Mrs. T

Chapter Nine

YOUR LOVE FILLS MY HEART, LORD!

. . . A FRESH DISCOVERY
OF HOW MUCH GOD
LOVES . . .

It is my prayer that this chapter will fill your heart with joy and hope as you read passages from teens who share testimonies of God's unfailing love. Through their perspectives, you will be taken on a journey that will lead to a fresh discovery of how much God loves each and every one of us. You might also be challenged to love those around you with God's love. Let this chapter nourish you as you focus on love.

. . . *I CLEARLY REMEMBER FEELING GOD'S PRESENCE SURROUNDING ME . . .*

Although I have been going to church on Sunday every week since I was a toddler, and even attending a religious school since kindergarten, only recently have I truly come to recognize and appreciate God's love in my life. While walking home from the bus stop about two years ago, I remember deciding to take the more scenic route through the woods back to my house. It was on that warm spring afternoon that I clearly remember feeling God's presence surrounding me. The warm sun on my face, the sweet breeze rustling the trees, and the birds chirping nearby filled me with a sense of peace, warmth, and joy that was none other than God's amazing love. From that day on, God's love has been a large part of my everyday life, and most importantly, my decision-making.

Seeing God and His presence in all of creation, especially my family, friends, teachers, and even complete strangers, has caused me to take a second look at how I treat others. Also, now every time I am about to make an important decision, whether it's contemplating whether to go to a party where I know drinking will be prevalent or even just deciding what to buy for lunch, I ask myself which choice would be thanking God for His unwavering love. I have come to realize that appreciating God's love is probably one of the best ways to show Him how thankful I really am. Respecting others, ourselves, and all of nature is a way everyone can feel God's love and show thanks. Besides clearly experiencing God's love through creation, I also believe that God's love is the warm feeling you experience after helping another individual. By realizing all beings are created in the image and likeness of God, when you help out another person in any way, you understand you are also sharing and professing your love for God. Therefore, as a result of God showering us with His love, we are able to discover this love within the core of our very beings.

THEA, 17

. . . GOD LOVES ME
EVEN WHEN EVERYONE ELSE
SEEMS NOT TO CARE . . .

God is love. When teenagers look at this phrase, we usually say, "Yeah, right." We don't believe in it because we have always been told that if we pray, God will always answer us and give us whatever we pray for. However, we don't realize that God grants us our petitions in many different ways. I don't consider myself an incredibly religious person. I believe in God, but I have lots of doubts about my faith. When something goes wrong, I blame the whole world for it; I blame God, too. But during times when everything seems to go wrong, like when I get in a fight with my parents and it seems like no one can help me, I turn to God and just talk to Him. Sometimes, I even go to church, and it just helps me get over my problems. When I sit in church, I feel safe and comfortable, and I know that God is with me. Then no one is yelling at me; I am just sitting quietly, thinking things over and over again, and I realize that God loves me even when everyone else seems not to care. I know then that with His help I can get over my problems much faster. Knowing that God always loves me helps me appreciate things and people around me, and this gives me confidence that He is always there for me no matter what happens.

JILL, 17

. . . I THOUGHT MY OWN DAD WAS LIKE GOD . . .

When I was really little, I thought my dad was like God. Every night I would ask him what the weather would be like the next day, and he said he would make the weather what he felt it should be. He would say, "Well, let's see. I think it should snow tomorrow, don't you?" This would happen every night, and in the morning, guess what? There would be snow! No matter the morning, rain, wind, snow, or sunshine, he was always right. When I got older, I realized that my dad did this out of his love for me. Then it hit me. If my dad loved me this much, and in my child's eyes he was God-like, then God's love must be really amazing! If my own dad could love me like he does, then God's love for me must be beyond my understanding—much like my dad's "control" of the weather!

TOREY, 14

I NEVER ASKED GOD
FOR HIS HELP . . .

In the past three years, I have had more worthwhile experiences than in the rest of my life put together. Along with new experiences, I have been influenced with new ideas and feelings from the people I am surrounded by. I have felt what it is to be a success and what it is to be a failure. I have known happiness and sadness, and I have known hope and despair. In the middle of all these feelings and experiences, I began to be confused about life in general. My freshman year, I entered high school knowing only three people. I was scared I wouldn't be cool enough or smart enough or pretty enough to fit in with everyone. I tried so hard to be myself, but I often found myself acting differently just to be like everyone else.

This way of life continued during my sophomore and junior years. I would laugh at things I did not find funny. I agreed with things I did not believe in. I did just about anything to try to make others like me. I had a few close friends with whom I could be myself, but in school or at parties I had to be careful how I acted. Oftentimes I would ask myself why I felt I had to be this way. Why couldn't I be happy with who I was? I never asked God for His help during my time of need. I suppose I never really thought He would be any help to me. He was there the whole time, though, and I know that now.

In October of my senior year, I went on an overnight retreat. I was glad I got to miss two days of school, but I never expected it to have such an enormous impact on my life. My perspective on my family and friends, school and life in general was totally changed. I got in touch with God and myself in a way I never imagined was possible. I began to realize that in the past three years, I had not done anything for myself. Everything I ever did or said was for someone else. I finally realized that I did not have to do that. I know that my family will support me in anything that I choose to do with my life. I know who my true friends are, and they are all I need. I don't regret the past few years because I learned from all my mistakes. When I wasn't even looking for God, I found Him. I know that He will remain in my heart and love me forever. He is a powerful guiding force, and I feel fortunate to have realized it.

SHAYNE, 18

GOD'S LOVE IS THAT UNSEEN, BUT NOT UNFELT, PRESENCE . . .

God so loves the world that He gave Jesus, His Son, to us. God gives unconditional love to all people, regardless of what they have or have not done. God's love is visible in all of nature, the birds, the trees, the sunshine. God's love is that unseen, but not unfelt, presence that makes the world a better place.

JOSÉ, 17

MY DAD WAS AN ALCOHOLIC . . .

I never really had a good relationship with God when I was younger, probably because He wasn't introduced to me by my parents. My dad was an alcoholic. He used to drink while he was at work, and then come home and be very violent. My brother and I used to sit through the horrible fights every night, and it would usually get to the point where we (my mother, brother, and I) had to leave and get a hotel room. If you asked me two years ago how many nights I actually slept in my own bed, the answer would probably be no more than ten. Sometimes, my mom wouldn't leave the house, and I would call a family friend. She would have to come and get us. I honestly believe this person is an angel in disguise. Through her, I began to have a relationship with God. She introduced me to Him and kept me headed in the right direction, even though all I was seeing was violence. Through her, God kept love in my heart instead of hate. He also gave me the strength to persevere. I know now that God has been with me every step of the way. My dad and mom divorced, which was for the best in our situation, and my

dad finally got the help he needed. I wouldn't want anyone to go through what I have, but maybe with the love
God has given me, someday I can use my experiences to
help other people.

ROSLYN, 14

AUTHOR'S NOTE: Please remember that should violence ever
occur in your home, it is imperative to seek help. Talk to someone you trust who can lead you to resources to keep you safe.
Also, keep in mind that if you are living with an addict, organizations such as Al-Anon or Alateen (1-888-4-AL-ANON/1-888-
425-2666) can be helpful in providing support and guidance.

I GUESS GOD CAN SORT OF BE CONSIDERED THE FIRST ETERNAL OPTIMIST . . .

We humans, with our faulty conscience and moral failings, have messed up so many times that you'd think God would have just washed His hands of us a while ago. He didn't, though, and probably never will. Can you understand that kind of patience and love? I mean, I can get pretty mad at small occurrences, never mind a world war or any other numerous instances where the human race has been less than perfect. I mean, can you imagine how stupid and misguided war must seem to God? It entails thousands of His supposedly intelligent creatures blowing each other's heads off . . . for what? A chunk of land or a couple more meaningless pieces of paper or bars of yellow metal? If I tally up my day's actions, the ones I perform are usually done more for bad intentions or wrong ones. But I haven't been struck down yet, so I guess God is willing to forgive me and keep His unshaking patience. I guess God can sort of be considered the first eternal optimist. He is always ready to forgive us and is never negative in His view of our wavering world.

HECTOR, 17

I WAS A REBEL CHILD . . .

My life has been moderately hard. I think many teens would say the same about their lives. But I have not always lived my life the way I do now. I used to make very bad decisions. I used to cuss like a banshee. I used to all-out rebel and disrespect my mother. I was a rebel child, and I did not live my life in a way acceptable to God. And yet, if you had asked me during this time if I was a Christian, I would have said yes. But I think I would have been wrong. I've learned that you cannot just talk the talk; it is also important to walk the walk. I think my youth group leader helped me realize this.

My youth pastor took me directly under his wing and treated me like his son. He had a very strong belief about never cussing, as did the youth group. I feel that this is valid in that it can stunt your spiritual growth. The Bible says, "From the overflow of the heart, the mouth speaks," and I did not want such disgusting things in my heart. Now I rarely ever cuss. My youth pastor also showed me unconditional love, which after a month or two, I picked up on and started to attempt to treat others the way he treated me. It really isn't all that hard, if you try. He taught me how to make right decisions by going to God and asking for His advice and always listening to His voice. If anything, this is one of the more difficult things for teens to do. He also showed me verses in the Bible about disrespecting your parents. He taught me how to deal with my parents and how to love them. That carried over to how I treated other people. If there is one thing I have always had trouble with, it is the command to "love all." What a command! How can you love people who treat you badly? I can tell you the answer to that. It is impossible for us to attempt to love all people on our own. You have to give it to God! He will give you the love in your heart to spread to all others. Then He will give you patience, love, kindness, selflessness, and compassion, all of which I have found you need to love all others. Even though people are very cruel to me at times, even though I may not like them in the least, I will always try to love them. There are many times that I find I cannot do some of these demanding tasks, and usually those are the times I am trying to do it on my own. You always have to give it to God. That doesn't mean you don't have to do some work in your life; it just means He will give you the power to do that work.

BRYAN, 15

. . . HIS LOVE-FILLED FACE . . .

Behind the smile, the face, the clothes
Is a girl whose life has completely froze.
A mask is what she hides behind,
The answers to life she cannot find.
Everything passes; a hazy, cloudy blur.
She wonders why this is all happening to her.
Self conscious about everything from head to toe,
Trusting no one, she will not let her feelings show.
Everyone else seems happy, so fixed, and so real.
She wonders why her own wounds will not heal.
Her life seemed unwritten, unscripted, unplanned.
She walked around aimlessly, ignoring God's hand.
He patiently waited for her day after day,
but felt His heart ache when she walked the other way.
He watches her search from place to place,
Ignoring His scarred hands and feet, His love-filled face.
For her He died, yes, He loved her that much.

He waits for the day she'll pray for His healing touch.

Until then, He will wait, yes, He will wait.

He wants her to find Him before it's too late.

He'll stay by her side, help her up when she falls.

Until she discovers, finally for herself, the great love of all.

ALEYSHA, 17

HIS LOVE FOR EACH OF US IS BEYOND COMPREHENSION . . .

I know that God is always there for me, waiting for me to speak to Him. He wants me to tell Him anything, everything! I can pray to God at any time. During the day, I find myself praying for guidance whenever I need it. If I need a listening ear, I know He will be there for me. After I pray, I am careful to stop for a few minutes and listen for an answer. God will answer your prayers! His love for each of us is beyond comprehension. When I feel this love, it surrounds me like a blanket, and I am peaceful inside. Nothing else matters. I put all my trust in God, and He showers me with unconditional love in return. It's a great system. In this day and age, it's easy to get pulled into the pressures of society. My faith in God keeps me steadfast on my journey to eternal life in His presence. It's a great feeling being loved. With God on my side, I know that I am never alone.

JESSI, 14

MY LIFE IS VERY HARD,
BUT . . .

Sometimes things in my life become completely over-whelming, and there seems to be nowhere to turn. Things get so bad and lonely, I feel as though no one would notice if I was gone. On days like these, the only one I have to turn to is God. I am forced to think about the value of my life, knowing that God has given me so much. God gave me gifts that I have to offer to other people. God has made me a strong person with all of my battles. My life is very hard, but someone out there has it worse. After every problem, it gets better. It helps me keep my faith.

I have to trust in God. I haven't given up on me, and though many other people think I am too messed up, God won't give up on me either. I know that I have respect, faith, and trust in God, so He must have those things in me. No matter how hard my life gets, I will always have someone to turn to, someone who loves me. Even on the days when I feel so completely worthless, I know that God is watching over me. And I know I can't give in. God gave me my life as a gift from Him, so I have to respect it. God gave me something of His own, and even though I feel like some days His choice for my life was unfair, I know by choosing this path for me I will have a better life, full of lessons and truths sent from God. I have to respect the gift He has given me. God gave me a life where I know people's struggles. I know what pain is, and I can offer comfort to the people who don't have the faith that I do. My life has given me such a greater respect for people and how they live, act, and learn. God has a greater plan for me, and I can't give up, or I would be giving up on God and His love for me. Besides, I find great hope in knowing that someone will always love me: God!

JORDI, 15

OUR MOM SENT US AWAY TO PROTECT US FROM OUR DAD . . .

I have faced much fear and discomfort in my early child-hood years. One day, when I was seven, the school day had just ended, and my sister and I were called to the office by intercom. Once we got there, we were given books to read before the principal came in to talk with us. At the time, we were very scared because we thought we were in trouble. The principal felt really bad about telling us of the situation, but he got through it. He told us that our parents weren't home and that we had to go to a fun place where we would meet lots of new people. Later that day, we were taken to a foster-care center. We were frightened to find out that our parents couldn't take care of us anymore. Our mom sent us away to protect us from our dad because he was an alco-holic, used illegal drugs, and was abusive. Our dad some-times chased us with a vacuum or told us to walk around the block with a bottle of beer and not to come back until it was empty. When we walked around the block with the beer, I threw it in a neighbor's garbage can because I didn't want to end up like my dad. We tried to avoid our dad as much as we could once we noticed the danger.

When we got to the foster-care center, God gave me courage, and I knew He was watching over me. I made many new friends who took me warmly by the hand and helped me to move on and start my new life like the others there. I didn't keep my friends for very long, though, because after about a week, my sister and I were chosen to leave with our first foster parents. Later, I was sent to three more foster homes. After a couple of years, God finally led us to our adoption family. He picked the perfect family for my sister and me because we do many things as a family and enjoy being one. I was allowed to see my mom one last time before I was adopted, and I was and still am grateful for the moment. I was afraid that I would never see her after that scary day after school. The chance to see her again gave me that feeling that she still did really love us. When I turn nineteen, I plan on finding out where my mom is so I can see her again and catch up on all the years that have passed between us.

I went through some rough times in my younger life, and you might think I would be angry at God about all that I was put through. But I don't blame God because I don't believe it was His fault. Seven years ago, to tell the truth, I never thought about God being there with me. I look back now and realize He was with me the whole time. I was disappointed in myself that I didn't think about Him being there when I was little, but I know now that you don't have to think about God for Him to be there for you or for Him to love you. He showed His love for me by sending me on a better path. This was the scariest experience in my younger years, but God was and is still always there to help me. God overwhelmed me with His love, and even though I didn't notice it at the time, I sure do now.

COLIN, 14

. . . THEY CARRIED OUT
GOD'S LOVE . . .

Comfort, help, and friendship are all aspects of God's love. At one point in my life, confusion and pain were the only feelings I endured. The death of my brother, whom I was closer to than anyone else on this Earth, destroyed my senses of reality and understanding. His death left me an emotional and psychological mess. At first, a sense of betrayal was all I felt toward God. But that soon changed. Almost instantly after my brother died, friends began offering themselves to my family and me. These acts of kindness, compassion, and love really helped me, not to understand, but to accept and grow. Friends from my church best represent God to me. I feel that they carried out God's love. By showing compassion and love through these people, God touched my heart and helped me heal.

AARRON, 17

"T" TALK

Isolated. Empty. Incomplete. These are such sad and lonely words. Yet, I have heard so many teens use them when referring to their lives or to how they feel inside. My cousin, Sion, has used these words to describe his teenage years as well.

If you were to ask Sion's peers, they likely would have told you that he had the ideal life, because when they looked at Sion's family and his lifestyle, they thought he had it all. They watched Sion's stepmom cheer louder and longer than anyone else at every one of Sion's football games. They knew that Sion's dad was one of the few who would give his son a big bear hug in front of everyone and say, "I love you." His friends were aware that Sion had a nice home, a hot car, and a little extra spending money. They also knew that Sion's family spent time together on fun vacations, snowboarding, waterskiing, and taking houseboat trips.

But what Sion's peers didn't see was that his biological

mom and dad were both recovering addicts. They divorced when Sion was a child. Sion's dad remarried an extraordinary woman, and together they did their best to raise Sion and his younger brothers with love and understanding. Yet for Sion, something was still missing. Perhaps it was the addiction issues that had plagued his family throughout his childhood. Or he thinks it could have had something to do with the deaths of his best friends in a car accident—a car in which Sion was supposed to be riding. Regardless of the reason, an emptiness grew inside his heart.

In his early teens, Sion chose to fill that void with temporary pleasures. He began to drink and experiment with drugs. Marijuana became Sion's drug of choice. Soon he was getting high every day, throughout the day. Even knowing that he was at risk for becoming an addict because of his family's history with addiction, Sion still chose to use. In spite of knowing better, Sion also rationalized his use by telling himself that pot wasn't a hardcore drug. So he smoked a lot, slept a lot, and in between tried to maintain a somewhat "normal" teen existence. The reality of the situation, however, was that as much as using alcohol and drugs may have given Sion momentary pleasure, the feeling never lasted.

It was not until recently, when Sion discovered God's unending love, that he realized that his short-lived vices were meaningless. He had gone to church in the past, and he had always believed in God, but his prior spiritual experiences had been routine and insignificant. For some reason, even unbeknownst to Sion, this time it was different. It may have been something the pastor said, or perhaps it was simply that Sion was tired of living life as he was, but this time as he sat in church beside his brother, he experienced the feeling of his heart overflowing with the unconditional love of God. Only in that moment did he understand that the path he had chosen previously only nourished his feeling of emptiness. When Sion smoked pot, he could fill his lungs with smoke and hold it there until he began to feel the high taking hold. This high may have carried him a few moments or even a few hours, but in the end this feeling was only temporary. Now, with thanksgiving, Sion understands that God's love can carry him for a lifetime. He doesn't need drugs or alcohol because he has the love of God. His love is unconditional. God loves without reservation or restriction, despite one's faults or flaws. His love is unchanging, everlasting, and pure. Can you imagine this type of love?

Picture this: A teenager goes to a party with his friends. His intention is to hang out, have fun, and stay sober. However, everyone is having such a good time that when a beer is offered to him, he decides, "Why not?" Ultimately, that one beer turns into many more. Soon he knows that he's gone too far. His dad had always said that although he hoped his son would never put himself in such a situation, if he ever did, his dad would be only a phone call away. So the teen calls home and asks his dad to pick him up. He waits nervously, worried that his dad will be mad and ground him 24/7, but more than that the teen fears that he will disappoint his dad. Yet, when his father arrives, he puts his arm around his son and walks him to the car. Once inside, the teen drops his head in his hands, and with tears in his eyes says, "Dad, I'm so sorry. I don't know what I was thinking." His dad reaches over and touches his face so that their eyes meet, and he says, "Son, I love you so much. Even though I may not approve of your drinking tonight, and despite the fact that there will be consequences for your choices, I am so proud that you called me."

Can you conceive the amount of love and grace that filled the car that night? Not to mention the abundance of love that was felt in each of their hearts. I find it amazing to consider that if a mortal father can love his child that much, then our heavenly Father is capable of a love beyond our wildest dreams! From a teen perspective, I would think that God's love would be one of the most incredible experiences in the world.

Because God's love is offered without strings attached, He loves you for who you are, not how you look or what you do. God loves you regardless of whether your hair is dyed or if you have a tattoo or an obscure piercing. Likewise, He doesn't require that you wear certain clothes or shoes to be accepted by Him. Name brands mean nothing to God. He doesn't love you because you get good grades or because you are a fantastic musician or a great skater. You see, who you are on the outside doesn't matter to God. He loves you because of who you are on the inside. God loves you because you are YOU!

Given such, I have spoken with numerous teenagers who have expressed that they feel unworthy of God's love. Please know that no one is worthless in God's eyes. This is why He sent Jesus to live among us and die for us. It is also why He gave us the Holy Spirit to live within each of us. God's love for us is that strong. Rely on faith to connect your desire for a love so real with the blessing of God's offering. Open your heart to God, and let Him fill you with His love.

Considering God's gift of love to us, wouldn't you think that we should love one another in kind? The obvious answer would seem to be simple, yet the reality is quite bleak. Think about your school environment. There is so much judgment and jealousy that exists at most schools. Teens are labeled based on the way they dress, what they are involved in, or where they live. People tease and discriminate on the premise of what someone looks like or who they hang out with. Sadly, no love can be found in this behavior. Consequently, the ultimate outcome causes heartache and anger and can force the judged into depression, isolation, or rebellion. Where is the love in this? Why must we judge? Aren't we all similar on the inside? Don't we all crave love and understanding? Don't we all wrestle with our emotions when faced with difficult life situations? If so, then why not focus on love?

If you are thinking, Yeah, why not? then we should probably attempt to understand the meaning of love. Many would describe love as an emotion that one feels. Being "in love" may actually be described as a strong emotion that makes your heart feel as if it is going to burst from the sheer pleasure and overwhelming joy that encompasses the feeling. At the same time, apostle Paul proposes that true love is fundamentally an action rather than an emotion. He writes, in essence, that if you were to use the model of Christ's love, you would be kind and patient. You would not be jealous or envious of others. If you were to act out of pure love, you would not be rude or conceited. Therefore, boasting would definitely be out. You would need to hold your temper and not keep track of the wrongs done to you. Your actions would always show honesty and truth. You would not do anything that would be considered evil or corrupt. You would always protect and trust people, including your parents. And you would always keep trying with a hopeful heart, even when utterly frustrated or confused.

I realize that it may seem almost impossible to even attempt to love others in such a way, especially on days when you wake up on the wrong side of the bed or get into a huge fight with your parents or friends. The good news is that God knows that you are going to have bad days. He understands your imperfections. After all, He created you. Who better to understand you than the Lord? So if you are confused or feeling inept about how to love others in such a Christ-like way, take your concerns to God. Let Him guide you and teach you. Reflect on Jesus's model as the perfect example of how to love. During the days that Jesus walked the Earth, He was nonjudgmental and accepting of people, especially those who were considered outcasts. He took time to meet the needs of others, but He also took care of Himself. If He needed time alone to pray, He made sure that His time was uninterrupted. In this way, He reminds us that acting out of love means loving ourselves as well. He also prayed for people with utter compassion and complete conviction. We, too, can love in this way. I feel sure that if we each take a step to love each other as God loves us, such love would enrich our family relationships, friendships, and even our school atmosphere. For that matter, our world would flourish with love and peace.

On the other hand, you may feel that loving others comes naturally to you. Perhaps, instead, you struggle with a need to be loved. Do you feel alone in this world? Do you ever wonder if anyone really cares about you? I have spoken with many teens who have felt this way. Some have been homeless, others abused. Several felt neglected by parents who had to work long hours to put food on the table. There are numerous teenagers who feel unloved because their mom and dad have divorced, and now their parents' time and energy are focused on dating and making ends meet. This isn't to say that the parents of these teens don't love their kids, because undoubtedly they do; it is just that in their current situation, the teens may not feel loved. Regardless of why you might feel alone or unloved, know that God does love you. He is simply waiting for you to accept His love. Considering this, you may be wondering how to recognize God's love.

Remarkably, God showers us with His love in so many ways. When a stranger smiles at us and brightens our day, God's love is touching us through that person. When a friend shows us kindness, we can feel God's love. When we observe the beauty in nature, we can thank God for loving us so much to give us peace in the warm sun and hope in the majesty of the mountains. His love is even evident in joy that you feel in your heart when that hot girl or guy that you've been subtly flirting with all week flirts back. (Okay, so maybe your hormones have something to do with that one, but still.) When it comes down to it, God showers us with these visions and experiences so that we may have evidence of how much He cares.

With God's love will come a joy and fulfillment that you may have never felt before. If you have already accepted God's love in your life, then you know what I mean. My cousin Sion told me that when he first experienced God's love, he learned that there was a difference between happiness and joy. He found happiness to be temporary. A person can easily be happy one moment and sad the next. However, joy is eternal. It lives in your heart through God's love and stays forever. I pray that you find joy in God's love, because the power of His love can change the world. I encourage you to embrace, share, and celebrate the love of the Lord!

Mrs. T

Chapter Ten

LET ME SHARE YOUR HOPE

GOD IS HOPE . . .

Throughout this book, you have read about the life experiences of a multitude of teens. They have taken you on a journey of their trials and tragedies, joys and triumphs. Some of the stories that you read may have touched your heart and brought tears to your eyes. Others might have made you smile or laugh. At the same time, I hope that many passages taught you lessons and encouraged you in your faith. But, when all is said and done, it comes down to this chapter. I say this because no matter what you experience in life, if you look to the Lord, He will grant hope to your heart every day! As teens will express in this final chapter, God is hope, and He desires to share it with you!

Mrs. T

GOD'S LOVE IS NEVER ENDING . . .

Ever had a constant romance in your life, and then all of a sudden the romance ends and you are left in the dust? How do you feel? Do you feel angry, betrayed, alone? Well, there is one who will never leave you alone. When you think no one cares about you or even loves you, you are wrong. There is one who loves you with all of His heart and will never forsake you, ever! His name is Jesus, and over two thousand years ago He walked this Earth, died, was nailed to a cross, and resurrected just to save someone like YOU. That may sound way too extreme, and it might scare you in some ways, but He died to give you life. As John 3:16 says: "For God so loved the world that He gave His one and only Son, that whoever believes in Him shall not perish but have eternal life." God's love is never ending. If you don't know God, please find a church, talk to a pastor or ask a friend who does know God for help. I assure you that they will help you meet God. Please take advantage of this glorious miracle and embrace the love that is waiting for you in God's arms!

WRENNA, 15

HE GAVE US LIFE, SO WHY NOT BELIEVE . . .

I believe in God for many reasons. He can help us so much. Ever since day one, I have had faith in God, and each year it grows stronger. If I somehow got pulled away from Him, I would be blind and lost. He will help anyone, if you just ask Him with sincerity. He loves us all, and He wants to help us. He gave us life, so why not believe in Him? When I am scared, nervous, or faced with a hard decision, I turn to Him, and He leads me in the right direction. Not only do I ask for His guidance in those situations, but I do it every day. Sometimes I just ask Him to keep me strong, so I can resist the temptations of the world. He has always been there for me, and I know that He will be there for you if you just ask Him.

ALICE, 14

YOU CAN LET HIM IN BY OPENING YOUR HEART . . .

God will help anyone at any time. He doesn't judge your past but wants you to have a good future. He also provides you with the hope that He will guide you out of troubles or misfortunes. He will do this because He loves you, and if you let Him in, He will do anything for you. You can let Him in by opening your heart to Him, not asking for things, but thanking Him for being present in your life. If you just acknowledge Him, He will help you and provide hope for your life.

COREY, 15

HE WILL ALWAYS
BE THERE . . .

It's really hard for me to tell you why I am a Christian. It is not just a thing you do or say, but a way of life. It is indescribable. When you truly have Jesus as your Lord and Savior, you will never be alone again. You will never have to make a decision by yourself again. He will always be there for you. I know lots of people who think faith or religion is just a bunch of rules to live by, but it's not. It is more than that. It truly is a way to have love in your life by living every day of your life for God.

GRACE, 14

I WANT TO BE WHAT HE WANTS ME TO BE . . .

As I look to the heavens I know He is there,

Showering me, giving me His love and all of His care.

Every day I wake up and thank God for life,

He's helped me through so much, all of my pain and my strife.

I feel God inside me; I know He is there to show me the way,

To guide me, to love me, to help me through every single day.

Jesus is there above me, and I thank Him for all He has done.

He is the Savior, the Messiah; it is my heart He has won.

The emotions and feelings I have for God are too strong to express in words.

He has shown me the world and has given me life; the true things that matter from Him I have learned.

I want to be what He wants me to be; it is Jesus that I
    see.

I get down on my knees and say thanks that my Lord
    loves me.

I have my faith, oh Lord, and it comes straight from my
    heart.

It is this faith in You that from my body shall never part.

And I say to You, Lord, that no matter what happens, no
    matter what I do,

I hope You are listening, oh Lord, because God,
    I love You!

ANTONIO, 16

. . . WE CAN'T JUST GIVE UP WHEN THINGS SEEM DIFFICULT . . .

Having hope in God is similar to having confidence in a friend. He doesn't impose Himself on you. He'll listen to you no matter what. He'll give you support during difficult times. He'll carry you when you can't go on. But I also understand that it is easy to lose hope. Looking at the world, and all the bad things that have happened and are happening, I can see how some people could lose hope in God. We just have to remember that God would never give us anything we couldn't handle. Most of the problems we have today, such as hunger, poverty, and war, can all be improved if we just worked together to do something about them. There is enough food to feed everyone in the world. There are enough materials to build decent houses for everyone in the world without being destructive to the planet. There is enough good in the world to stop all war and bring everlasting peace. We just have to realize that we can't just give up when things seem difficult. We can't just think that somebody else will take care of it. Most of all, we have to realize that it *is possible*. We just have to care enough, realize our hope in God, and go out and make it happen. Remember, with God anything is possible. In this sometimes hopeless world, to have hope is to have God. Remember this saying, "Don't lose hope, for like the stars that come out at night, the light of God shines brightest in the dark."

TARYN, 17

MY FAITH IN GOD HAS GIVEN ME A SENSE OF DIRECTION AND HOPE . . .

Teenage years are probably some of the most difficult times to go through. There is peer pressure to do things that may not appeal to you. There is the fear of what people might think of you if you don't fit in. There is a great amount of confusion about friendships and relationships. Although things sometimes seem so hard, I have learned through experience that if you have hope in God and believe that He will guide you through things, it will be okay. I realize through my faith in God that even in the toughest times, I know that someone else in the world has it worse than me. I should be happy for what God did give me and learn to accept my hardships. My faith in God has given me a sense of direction and hope. It has taught me to stand strong in my beliefs and values, and not worry about what others think because God is the one who truly knows me. So stay positive toward your own values, and your hope in God will help you through.

DANI, 16

JESUS WILL BE WITH YOU EVERY STEP OF THE WAY . . .

When you feel alone or abandoned, hated or forgotten, don't give up hope that things will get better! When life gets bad enough that you want to give up, God is with you! He will always be with you. He loves you so much that He gave His one and only Son to die for you, so you wouldn't have to spend eternity away from Him. All you have to do is accept Jesus as your Lord and Savior, and ask Him for forgiveness. So, if things are tough, remember: carry on and head straight for the light at the end of whatever tunnel you are in. Jesus will be with you every step of the way, guiding you away from temptation, and protecting you from evil. When you feel the weakest, that is when you can be your strongest if you just look to the Lord. Don't turn your back on Jesus because He will never turn His back on you!

CONNOR, 14

HE IS THE LITTLE LIGHT
OF HOPE . . .

God is always there with you. He is the little light of hope getting you through the worst days of your life.

MAYSON, 18

. . . A BONFIRE OF HOPE . . .

I will always remember the moment when my sixth-grade teacher appointed a boy in our class to join my reading group. He loudly objected, "I don't want to be in this stupid group because they're not smart enough." He sneered at the teacher and refused to move. This was the first time my learning disability was broadcast to my friends. At that moment, I visualized the chain of gossip going from this class and throughout the school. My thoughts got uglier as class dragged on; I felt terrible. I tried to sneak out of the classroom so no one would see me. Luckily, it was near the end of the day, so I only suffered a short time until I could share the incident with my mom, who was waiting for me outside. If ever there lives a bonfire of hope, it is in my mother. To me, she is God's channel of it. I think we don't recognize that sometimes. God uses people in our lives to bless us with hope. For me, that person is my mom. After I explained my sadness and worry to her, sparks flew. She set about to right the situation, and a line of support quickly came to my aid.

At bedtime each night, I thank God for everything. Well, not quite everything. . . . Why did I have to be born with a learning disability? At this point, I don't know how to tell Him "thanks" for that. I can only hope that someday I will understand. And as my mom always points out: Life can be a whole lot worse, so never give up hope!

EDDIE, 15

. . . GOD WILL ALWAYS FORGIVE YOU . . .

I know how much God helps me every day, and I want people, including you, to have the same feeling that I do . . . that someone cares for you, that you have someone to talk to when you're feeling bad. The Lord is always there for you, and He loves you and forgives you even when you sin. In Psalm 23 it says: "The Lord is my shepherd . . . He restores my soul." I think the psalm means that God will always forgive you, and He will restore your mind and soul with good, not bad. If you already are a Christian, I just have one more thing to say: Share the Lord with people, and let them see His light through you, and how happy you are to have the Lord in your life!

ANGELICE, 14

GOD HAS BEEN THERE
FOR ME . . .

I was always brought up as a Christian. When I was born, my mom was a strong Christian and still is. I went to church with her as much as possible. When I was old enough to understand completely, I accepted God as my personal Lord and Savior. He has helped me through many things. The one specific event that God helped me through the most was the death of my brother. I mean, I still feel the pain of losing my only brother, but God reminds me that He has a plan for everything and that we will be reunited in heaven someday. God keeps me on the right path. When I am presented with a difficult situation, I go directly to Him. He guides me, just like a lost sheep. I rely on Him for everything, because without God, we are nothing.

So, what would I tell teens about Him? I would have to start by telling them that He can help you through all your problems—anything from relationships, school, family, friends, etc. Also, He will give you eternal life in heaven if you just believe in Him. People say that Christians miss out on all the good things—drinking, sex, all the fun—but I don't think so. By setting standards, God is just protecting you and showing that He cares very deeply for you. God has been there for me. He will be there for you, too.

JAY, 15

... A WONDERFUL FEELING
OF PEACE ...

I can't really pick out or define one specific area or category of God that means the most to me. He's been so involved in every single aspect of my life, especially recently. My life has been definitely better, more rich and joyful, since I've decided to let God in. First off, I guess, is guidance. My junior year has been extremely stressful, and sometimes I have trouble handling it. My anxiety bubbles over into other areas in my life, and my friends, family, and relationships always suffer. For a while, I might even get confused about God. Then something always happens to make it better. Maybe a song comes on the radio or a friend calls or a teacher spends a little extra time with me. Or even, for no reason at all, a wonderful feeling of peace comes over me. At times like this, I know God is guiding me and comforting me, saying, "It's going to be all right. Don't worry."

God has an awesome amount of patience, too. The number of times I've messed up or turned my back on Him is countless. Yet, there's always His love, beckoning me back. Because of this, I've realized that all of my guilt and sin can be washed away by God's love and patience. It's an awesome gift.

This sort of leads into my next point: God is grace. I feel so overwhelmed at times, and all of a sudden, I can literally feel His loving presence. And that's what grace is: God's forgiving and patient presence. If His grace is with you, you're okay. One time, I did some pretty bad stuff. I thought that I had hidden it pretty well from my parents, but I hadn't. They found out, and I was busted. My punishment was severe, but it fit the offense. However, I was inconsolable. All of these thoughts ran through my mind: "I'm a rotten kid." "Why am I even here?" "I'm a waste of air." "Nobody will ever trust me again." Basically, I was wallowing in self-pity. Then, I could suddenly sense this feeling of peacefulness, and I knew it was God's grace healing and consoling me.

When I was little, I used to say my prayers every night, regarding them more as an obligation than anything else. Then I started to realize what prayer is: not reciting rote passages as fast as you can so you won't go to hell, but being with God, hanging out with Him, if you will. I think over this last year, I've prayed more than ever before, in both ways, ritual and conversation. I've learned that God will answer your prayers. It might not always be in the way that you want, but God does listen and respond to you. All of these things I've talked about have one thing in common: my faith in God. It's central to everything in my life. I know that with Him, I can do anything. Like that church song goes: "If God is for us, who can be against us?" Give God a shot in your life. What have you got to lose?

TRAVIS, 16

ACTIONS DEFINITELY SPEAK LOUDER THAN WORDS . . .

All my life I have been raised a Christian. I have always gone to a religious school, and I attend church regularly. When compared to the society around me, I always considered myself to be a pretty devoted Christian. That view of myself drastically changed six months ago when I spent three weeks of my summer in a little village way up in the mountains of Haiti. In the village of Dessables, the people have virtually no material possessions, especially when compared to the environment I am accustomed to. Their houses are made of sticks, and they are lucky if they have an animal or two. Sometimes they will not eat for a week. Yet these people have incredible faith in God. The feeling you get when you are there in this presence is indescribable. I could truly see the face of God when I looked at these people. No matter what, they always put people before anything else. And even though we didn't speak the same language, I could always understand them. Actions definitely speak louder than words. They would go to church for the entire day on Sunday. And it was so full of life. Even though they didn't know where their next meal was coming from, they put their faith in God to watch over them. This experience has given me the strength to go beyond what is expected of me in my society as a Christian. I think of these people, and I know that I am doing good things, even when people question me as to why I put so much time and effort into God. It is not just for Him but also for me and all people of the world. I share this experience with you, hoping that you can see these people as an example and grow in your faith, too.

KAILYN, 17

. . . I AM SAVED . . .

Has anyone ever told you how great God is? Well, God is GREAT!! He is a strong and loving Father. He is the best. I believe in God because through this belief, I know that I am saved because of Jesus Christ, God's only Son. Faith is like a bridge between me and God. If I didn't have faith, it would be like not having air. My faith is a part of who I am. I am shaped around it. I am who I am because of what I believe. I believe in God, my only and everlasting Father; Jesus, my savior and everlasting friend; the Holy Spirit, my leader and everlasting guide. I am a Christian. I hope that you can believe in God, too!

BENITA, 16

"T" TALK

I have known many students who have touched my heart. Perhaps one may have a quick wit or a genuine compassion. Another may have had a tough life or seem hopelessly lonely. Regardless, different students have made lasting impressions upon me in various ways. One such student was Jason. What impressed me most about Jason was his natural ability to reach out to someone in need. It may have been with a touch, a smile, or even with a particular action. Jason always took it upon himself to look after others. However, after getting to know Jason, I realized that although he took initiative when it came to helping out his peers, he didn't seem to take time for himself. I asked him about it once, and he said that as far as he was concerned, his life really didn't matter. Jason told me about his parents' divorce, and how he'd like to live with his dad. However, in addition to his dad's verbally abusive behavior, he didn't seem to want Jason in his life. Jason explained that his relationship with his mom and siblings was falling apart. Jason felt that no one in his family listened to him or seemed to care about what he thought. This made him either depressed or extremely angry. He felt that he had no control over either of these feelings. To compound these emotions, Jason's best friend had recently died, and his girlfriend was in the process of being diagnosed with cancer. In his grief, his fear for her health, and his frustration within his own family, Jason felt he had no one to turn to.

Eventually, Jason confided in me that he felt an overwhelming sense of hopelessness. Feeling a bit helpless myself at the gravity of his situation, I asked him two questions. The first was if he would be open to counseling. He said that he'd tried that, but at this point didn't want to pursue it further. Second, I asked Jason if he had a spiritual faith to turn to during this difficult time in his life. Considering that he felt he had no one who would understand or listen to him, I thought that if he could turn to God, he wouldn't feel so alone. Yet, Jason wasn't so sure. He wondered if there really was a God, then why didn't He do something to show Jason that He cared? Why didn't He make Jason's life better? I asked Jason to consider that sometimes when we feel so discouraged or helpless, it is the perfect time to open our hearts to hope.

I remember leaving that conversation with Jason, wishing he could see that if only he could find faith in God, he would discover hope in his life, for I truly believe that our time on this Earth is a spiritual journey. I believe that everything that we experience in some way enhances our spiritual growth. That doesn't mean that God wants bad things to happen. But at the same time, I think that when bad things happen in our lives, God can enlighten us with precious life lessons, if only we choose to open our hearts to His teachings. Perhaps if Jason could understand this, he wouldn't feel so disheartened.

Hope. I talk to teens every day who have lost hope. Perhaps they have experienced a trial or tragedy in their lives, like some of the kids who wrote for this book. Maybe they have been abused or neglected. Perhaps someone in their lives died senselessly. More likely, though, the reason is a temporary problem that overwhelms them, like a breakup with a girlfriend or boyfriend or an inability to communicate with their parents. Yet regardless of the situation, a sense of hopelessness prevails. As Jason eventually discovered, though, the Lord can guide you out of your deepest despair.

To my surprise and answered prayers, that very summer Jason discovered God, and through his newfound faith, he encountered hope. Jason wrote me a letter that summer, telling me that he had been spending most of his time supporting his girlfriend through her radiation treatments. Yet, Jason had a different perspective this time. He said that he credited his new outlook to his girlfriend and her faith, and ultimately to God. Jason wrote, "I look at God, and I thank Him every day for the faith that He has given me and my girlfriend. The reason I have faith is because she had it, and I finally caught on. Having faith is like having this feeling in you that helps you know everything will be okay in the end." Jason told me that as he stood by his girlfriend throughout her time in the hospital, he had felt so much hope. He knew that she would beat the disease. At the same time, he understood that we all have obstacles we have to deal with in life. However, he felt that he would be able confront those placed upon his path because finding faith in God had led him to faith in himself. Jason didn't feel hopeless anymore. In fact, he said that if I were to ask him what the word "faith" means to him now, he would say it means "power"—the power to be able to take yourself out of situations that are hard and make them a little bit easier. Jason could not have done this alone, but with God by his side he felt that anything was possible.

If you are a Christian, you are probably smiling right now because you can identify with Jason. What a glorious feeling it is to share one's faith in the Lord. When your emptiness has been filled with God's love, when your doubt has been turned to belief by the Lord's comfort, you want other people to experience this feeling, too. Remember, though, that it is important to share God's hope without judging people for their resistance or skepticism. The best way to lead people to the Lord is with acceptance and love. Show them, by your actions, the peace and hope that they, too, can discover in Christianity. Be conscientious of their hesitation or doubt. If they seem to be pushing you away or avoiding you, it is possible that you are coming on too strong. Sometimes an overzealous Christian ends up alienating the very people he or she is trying to lead to Christ. Keep in mind that if you keep a humble heart and focus on God's love, He will guide you and help you to witness in a way that glorifies Him.

If you do not consider yourself a Christian or if you are trying to figure out this whole "God thing," know that discovery is part of your life journey. God is patiently knocking on the door to your heart. He doesn't have any desire to leave His place there because that is where He belongs. His sole purpose is to be available for you, to be yours. But He will not enter without an invitation. He wants the choice to be yours. Does that mean that if you invite Him in, you will hear fireworks and immediately feel "saved"? Maybe, but probably not. I can't tell you what you'll feel, because everyone's experience is unique. God touches each person's heart in a special way. Some people need time to get used to God living there and loving there. Others are ready to jump into a relationship with God right away. Regardless, I'll bet that if nothing else, you will feel just a tiny bit of peace enter your heart. God's promise to you is that, like a mustard seed growing, peace will grow into strength, love, and hope that exemplifies the glorious life found in the kingdom of God.

You may be wondering exactly how the Lord might provide someone with hope. I suppose He does so in a myriad of ways. Some teens have told me that feeling Christ's comforting presence has brought them peace. Others, like my friend Laura, have experienced a true miracle. Keep in mind that miracles are not beyond God's mighty power, and miracles undoubtedly bring hope. Many teenagers have shared that they discovered hope in an answered prayer. On the other hand, sometimes hope is found in an answer that is entirely different than we expected. Nonetheless, if you let God reside in your heart, a glimmer of hope will abide in endless splendor.

Still, I have had many teenagers say to me that they don't know how to invite God in; they don't know how to ask Him. The beauty of it is that there isn't a right or wrong way. You can simply use your own words to tell God that you want to turn your life over to Him. Ask God to reveal Himself to you in a way that you will understand. Tell Him that you want to love Him and receive His love in return. In your own words, express your sorrow for your past misdeeds and ask Him to guide you in your words and actions in the future. God will be so happy that you are opening your heart to Him that how you went about doing it will not matter to God at all.

Remember that when you feel you have nothing, you always have God. Sometimes, especially as teenagers, we are so focused on ourselves and our needs that it is difficult to let go of the hold we have on our problems and our lives and grab on to hope of God's love. Yet if you choose to let God hold you, your life will be lighter. There will be room in your heart for the Lord's joy. He is the Comforter and the Provider. He is the Maker and Counselor. God is the Lord of hope and the Giver of peace. If you don't have the answers and you are looking for hope, rely on the Lord. However, like Jason discovered, it is a matter of choice. You can turn from God, but in doing so you will be turning from His ability to provide you with the hope to persevere. So turn toward Him, and let God fill you with hope while you experience His joy, peace, courage, and love!

Mrs. T

APPENDIX 1:
SCRIPTURAL REFERENCES
(NEW INTERNATIONAL VERSION)

We have included several scriptural passages that apply
to the general content areas of *Chicken Soup for the Soul
Presents Teens Talkin' Faith*, but the Bible is literally full of
encouraging and enlightening verses. We encourage you
to take time to explore the Word of God on your own!

DOUBT

The Lord Himself goes before you and will be
with you; He will never leave you nor forsake
you.

—Deuteronomy 31:8

But when he asks, he must believe and not
doubt, because he who doubts is like a wave of
the sea, blown and tossed by the wind.

—James 1:6

Now, faith is being sure of what we hope for and
certain of what we do not see.

—Hebrews 11:1

Keep your lives free from the love of money and be content with what you have, because God has said, "Never will I leave you; never will I forsake you." So we say with confidence, "The Lord is my helper; I will not be afraid. What can man do to me?"

—Hebrews 13:5–6

A week later His disciples were in the house again, and Thomas was with them. Though the doors were locked, Jesus came and stood among them and said, "Peace be with you!" Then He said to Thomas, "Put your finger here; see my hands. Reach out your hand and put it into my side. Stop doubting and believe." Thomas said to Him, "My Lord and my God!" Then Jesus told him, "Because you have seen me, you have believed; blessed are those who have not seen and yet have believed."

—John 20:26–29

Immediately Jesus made the disciples get into the boat and go on ahead of Him to the other side, while He dismissed the crowd. After He had dismissed them, He went up on a mountainside by Himself to pray. When evening came, He was there alone, but the boat was already a considerable distance from land, buffeted by the waves because the wind was against it. During the fourth watch of the night Jesus went out to them, walking on the lake. When the disciples saw Him walking on the lake, they were terrified. "It's a ghost," they said, and cried out in fear. But Jesus immediately said to them: "Take courage! It is I. Don't be afraid." "Lord, if it's you," Peter replied, "tell me to come to you on the water." "Come," He said. Then Peter got down out of the boat, walked on the water and came toward Jesus. But when he saw the wind, he was afraid and, beginning to sink, cried out, "Lord, save me!" Immediately, Jesus reached out His hand and caught him. "You of little faith," He said, "why did you doubt?" And when they climbed into the boat, the wind died down. Then those who were in the boat worshiped Him, saying, "Truly You are the Son of God."

—Matthew 14:22–33

We live by faith, not by sight.

—2 Corinthians 5:7

"Everything is possible for him who believes."

—Mark 9:23

"For My thoughts are not your thoughts, neither are your ways My ways," declares the Lord. "As the heavens are higher than the Earth, so are My ways higher than your ways and My thoughts than your thoughts."

—Isaiah 55:8–9

Not only so, but we also rejoice in our sufferings, because we know that suffering produces perseverance; perseverance, character; and character, hope. And hope does not disappoint us, because God has poured out His love into our hearts by the Holy Spirit, whom He has given us.

—Romans 5:3–5

COURAGE AND STRENGTH

So we say with confidence, "The Lord is my helper; I will not be afraid. What can man do to me?"
—Hebrews 13:6

But You are a shield around me, O Lord; You bestow glory on me and lift up my head. To the Lord I cry aloud, and He answers me from His holy hill.
—Psalms 3:3-4

In my distress I called to the Lord; I cried to my God for help. From His temple He heard my voice; my cry came before Him, into His ears.
—Psalms 18:6

Wait for the Lord; be strong and take heart and wait for the Lord.
—Psalms 27:14

Since You are my rock and my fortress, for the sake of Your name lead and guide me.
—Psalms 31:3

The Lord is with me; I will not be afraid.
—Psalms 118:6

My soul is weary with sorrow; strengthen me according to Your word.
—Psalms 119:28

"Surely God is my salvation; I will trust and not be afraid. The Lord, the Lord, is my strength and

my song; He has become my salvation."
—Isaiah 12:2

"For I am the Lord, your God, who takes hold of your right hand and says to you, do not fear; I will help you."
—Isaiah 41:13

Not only so, but we also rejoice in our sufferings, because we know that suffering produces perseverance; perseverance, character; and character, hope. And hope does not disappoint us, because God has poured out His love into our hearts by the Holy Spirit, whom He has given us.
—Romans 5:3-5

I can do everything through Him who gives me strength.
—Philippians 4:13

Finally, be strong in the Lord and in His mighty power. Put on the full armor of God so that you can take your stand against the devil's schemes.
—Ephesians 6:10-11

Be on your guard; stand firm in the faith; be men of courage; be strong. Do everything in love.
—1 Corinthians 16:13-14

That is why, for Christ's sake, I delight in weaknesses, in insults, in hardships, in persecutions, in difficulties. For when I am weak, then I am strong.
—2 Corinthians 12:10

FORGIVENESS

Then Peter came to Jesus and asked, "Lord, how many times shall I forgive my brother when he sins against me? Up to seven times?" Jesus answered, "I tell you, not seven times, but seventy-seven times."

—Matthew 18:21–22

When you were dead in your sins and in the uncircumcision of your sinful nature, God made you alive with Christ. He forgave us all our sins, having canceled the written code, with its regulations, that was against us and that stood opposed to us; He took it away, nailing it to the cross.

—Colossians 2:13–14

In Him we have redemption through His blood, the forgiveness of sins, in accordance with the riches of God's grace that He lavished on us with all wisdom and understanding.

—Ephesians 1:7–8

Be kind and compassionate to one another, forgiving each other, just as in Christ God forgave you.

—Ephesians 4:32

For sin shall not be your master, because you are not under law, but under grace.

—Romans 6:14

Those controlled by the sinful nature cannot please God. You, however, are controlled not by the sinful nature but by the Spirit.

—Romans 8:8-9

Therefore, if anyone is in Christ, he is a new creation; the old has gone, the new has come!

—2 Corinthians 5:17

As far as the east is from the west, so far has He removed our transgressions from us.

—Psalms 103:12

The Lord our God is merciful and forgiving, even though we have rebelled against Him.

—Daniel 9:9

And when you stand praying, if you hold anything against anyone, forgive him, so that your Father in heaven may forgive you your sins.

—Mark 11:25

"Do not judge, and you will not be judged. Do not condemn, and you will not be condemned. Forgive, and you will be forgiven."

—Luke 6:37

Wash away all my iniquity and cleanse me from my sin.

—Psalms 51:2

If we confess our sins, He is faithful and just and will forgive us our sins and purify us from all unrighteousness.

—1 John 1:9

ANGER

Refrain from anger and turn from wrath; do not fret—it leads only to evil.

—Psalms 37:8

The Lord is compassionate and gracious, slow to anger, abounding in love. He will not always accuse, nor will He harbor His anger forever.

—Psalms 103:8–9

Trust in the Lord with all your heart and lean not on your own understanding; in all your ways acknowledge Him, and He will make your paths straight.

—Proverbs 3:5–6

A gentle answer turns away wrath, but a harsh word stirs up anger.

—Proverbs 15:1

Dear friends, do not be surprised at the painful trial you are suffering, as though something strange were happening to you. But rejoice that you participate in the sufferings of Christ, so that you may be overjoyed when His glory is revealed.

—1 Peter 4:12–13

[Love] is not rude, it is not self-seeking, it is not easily angered, it keeps no record of wrongs.

—1 Corinthians 13:5

For if you forgive men when they sin against you, your heavenly Father will also forgive you.

—Matthew 6:14

"In your anger do not sin": Do not let the sun go down while you are still angry.

—Ephesians 4:26

My dear brothers, take note of this: Everyone should be quick to listen, slow to speak and slow to become angry, for man's anger does not bring about the righteous life that God desires.

—James 1:19–20

TRUST

Trust in the Lord with all your heart and lean not on your own understanding; in all your ways acknowledge Him, and He will make your paths straight.

—Proverbs 3:5–6

Pay attention and listen to the sayings of the wise; apply your heart to what I teach, for it is pleasing when you keep them in your heart and have all of them ready on your lips. So that your trust may be in the Lord, I teach you today, even you.

—Proverbs 22:17–19

"Never will I leave you; never will I forsake you."

—Hebrews 13:5

Wait for the Lord; be strong and take heart and wait for the Lord.

—Psalms 27:14

Commit your way to the Lord; trust in Him and He will do this: He will make your righteousness shine like the dawn, the justice of your cause like the noonday sun.

—Psalms 37:5-6

Those who trust in the Lord are like Mount Zion, which cannot be shaken but endures forever.

—Psalms 125:1

Who among you fears the Lord and obeys the word of His servant? Let him who walks in the dark, who has no light, trust in the name of the Lord and rely on his God.

—Isaiah 50:10

The Lord will guide you always; He will satisfy your needs in a sun-scorched land and will strengthen your frame. You will be like a well-watered garden, like a spring whose waters never fail.

—Isaiah 58:11

"Do not let your hearts be troubled. Trust in God; trust also in Me. In My Father's house are many rooms; if it were not so, I would have told you. I am going there to prepare a place for you."

—John 14:1-2

PRAYER

Be joyful always; pray continually; give thanks in all circumstances, for this is God's will for you in Christ Jesus.

—1 Thessalonians 5:16–18

Devote yourselves to prayer, being watchful and thankful.

—Colossians 4:2

Come near to God and He will come near to you.

—James 4:8

"You will pray to Him, and He will hear you, and you will fulfill your vows."

—Job 22:27

"Because he loves Me," says the Lord, "I will rescue him; I will protect him, for he acknowledges My name. He will call upon Me, and I will answer him; I will be with him in trouble, I will deliver him and honor him."

—Psalms 91:14–15

The Lord is near to all who call on Him, to all who call on Him in truth.

—Psalms 145:18

"This, then, is how you should pray: 'Our Father in heaven, hallowed be Your name, Your kingdom come, your will be done on Earth as it is in heaven. Give us today our daily bread. Forgive us our debts, as we also have forgiven our debtors. And lead us not into temptation, but

deliver us from the evil one.'"
—Matthew 6:9-13

"Ask and it will be given to you; seek and you will find; knock and the door will be opened to you. For everyone who asks receives; he who seeks finds; and to him who knocks, the door will be opened."
—Matthew 7:7-8

"Again, I tell you that if two of you on Earth agree about anything you ask for, it will be done for you by my Father in heaven. For where two or three come together in my name, there am I with them."
—Matthew 18:19-20

Do not be anxious about anything, but in everything, by prayer and petition, with thanksgiving, present your requests to God. And the peace of God, which transcends all understanding, will guard your hearts and your minds in Christ Jesus.
—Philippians 4:6-7

Be joyful in hope, patient in affliction, faithful in prayer.
—Romans 12:12

Very early in the morning, while it was still dark, Jesus got up, left the house and went off to a solitary place, where He prayed.
—Mark 1:35

LOVE

Dear friends, let us love one another, for love comes from God. Everyone who loves has been born of God and knows God. Whoever does not love does not know God, because God is love.

—1 John 4:7–8

May the Lord make your love increase and over-flow for each other and for everyone else.

—1 Thessalonians 3:12

Love is patient, love is kind. It does not envy, it does not boast, it is not proud. It is not rude, it is not self-seeking, it is not easily angered, it keeps no record of wrongs. Love does not delight in evil but rejoices with the truth. It always protects, always trusts, always hopes, always perseveres.

—1 Corinthians 13:4–7

"For God so loved the world that He gave His one and only Son, that whoever believes in Him shall not perish but have eternal life."

—John 3:16

"A new command I give you: Love one another. As I have loved you, so you must love one another."

—John 13:34

Love the Lord your God with all your heart and with all your soul and with all your strength.

—Deuteronomy 6:5

The only thing that counts is faith expressing itself through love.

—Galatians 5:6

And this is my prayer: that your love may abound more and more in knowledge and depth of insight, so that you may be able to discern what is best and may be pure and blameless until the day of Christ, filled with the fruit of righteousness that comes through Jesus Christ— to the glory and praise of God.

—Philippians 1:9-11

I pray that out of His glorious riches He may strengthen you with power through His Spirit in your inner being, so that Christ may dwell in your hearts through faith. And I pray that you, being rooted and established in love, may have power, together with all the saints, to grasp how wide and long and high and deep is the love of Christ, and to know this love that surpasses knowledge—that you may be filled to the measure of all the fullness of God.

—Ephesians 3:16-19

Be completely humble and gentle; be patient, bearing with one another in love.

—Ephesians 4:2

FAITH AND HOPE

Consequently, faith comes from hearing the message, and the message is heard through the word of Christ.

—Romans 10:17

We have this hope as an anchor for the soul, firm and secure. It enters the inner sanctuary behind the curtain, where Jesus, who went before us, has entered on our behalf.

—Hebrews 6:19–20

By faith we understand that the universe was formed at God's command, so that what is seen was not made out of what was visible.

—Hebrews 11:3

We live by faith, not by sight.

—2 Corinthians 5:7

In Him and through faith in Him we may approach God with freedom and confidence.

—Ephesians 3:12

But as for me, I watch in hope for the Lord, I wait for God my Savior; my God will hear me.

—Micah 7:7

But those who hope in the Lord will renew their strength. They will soar on wings like eagles; they will run and not grow weary, they will walk and not be faint.

—Isaiah 40:31

And the peace of God, which transcends all understanding, will guard your hearts and your minds in Christ Jesus.

—Philippians 4:7

Not only so, but we also rejoice in our sufferings, because we know that suffering produces perseverance; perseverance, character; and character, hope. And hope does not disappoint us, because God has poured out His love into our hearts by the Holy Spirit, whom he has given us.

—Romans 5:3–5

Be joyful in hope, patient in affliction, faithful in prayer.

—Romans 12:12

I pray that you may be active in sharing your faith, so that you will have a full understanding of every good thing we have in Christ.

—Philemon 1:6

APPENDIX II:
RESOURCES AND HOTLINES

CHRISTIAN-BASED TEEN HELPLINES AND WEBSITES

Cook Ministries: www.cookministries.com
Custom Discipleship and other Cook resources provide the tools necessary for teens to become more like Christ.

The Covenant House: www.covenanthouse.org
or 1-800-388-3888
An agency that provides shelter and service to homeless and runaway youth.

Focus on the Family:
www.focusonthefamily.com or www.family.org
Family-focused organization that, through a variety of media venues, provides stories of faith and hope in God, family values, guidance, and support. Portions of the website and magazines specifically target teens.

National Youth Crisis Hotline: 1-800-HIT-HOME
(1-800-448-4663). Try 1-800-422-HOPE (4673).

A gospel-oriented hotline, from Youth Development International, for youth in crisis situations, including physical abuse, rape, runaways, pregnancy, drug use, and addiction, functioning with the purpose of restoring hope and the truth of Jesus Christ to American youth.

Youth Ministry Yellow Pages: www.youthworkers.net
Resources and referrals for Christian teens.

ABSTINENCE RESOURCES

National Abstinence Clearinghouse: www.abstinence.net and 1-800-767-6880
Central location where character, relationship, and abstinence programs, curricula, speakers, and materials can be accessed.

True Love Waits: www.lifeway.com/tlw/
Challenges teenagers and college students to make a commitment to sexual abstinence until marriage.

Why Wait? 1-800-588-9248
Abstinence encouragement from Josh McDowell Ministries.

GENERAL TEEN HELPLINES, INFORMATION LINES, AND WEBSITES

Al-Anon/Alateen: 1-800-356-9996 or
1-888-4-AL-ANON (1-888-425-2666)

Alcoholics Anonymous: See National Clearinghouse for Alcohol and Drug Information for a toll-free number or www.aa.org.

Eating Disorders Awareness and Prevention, Information and Referral Line: 1-800-931-2237

Grief Recovery Helpline: 1-800-445-4808

Narcotics Anonymous: See National Clearinghouse for Alcohol and Drug Information for a toll-free number or www.na.org.

National Clearinghouse for Alcohol and Drug Information: 1-800-788-2800

Will provide toll-free numbers for Alcoholics Anonymous and Narcotics Anonymous specific to the state in which one resides, as well as other toll-free numbers related to addiction issues.

National Clearinghouse on Child Abuse and Neglect: 1-800-394-3366

National Council on Alcoholism and Drug Dependence: 1-800-622-2255

National Directory of Children, Youth, and Family Services: 1-800-343-6681

National Drug Abuse Hotline: 1-800-662-4357

National Health Information Center: 1-800-336-4797

National Referral Network for Kids in Crisis: 1-800-KID-SAVE (1-800-543-7283)

National Referral Organization for Drug/Alcohol Treatment Programs: 1-800-454-8966

National Resource Center on Domestic Violence: 1-800-537-2238

National Runaway Switchboard: 1-800-621-4000

National Suicide Hotline: 1-800-SUICIDE (1-800-784-2433)

National Youth Crisis Hotline: 1-800-HIT-HOME
(1-800-448-4663)

Rape, Abuse and Incest National Network (RAINN):
1-800-656-HOPE (1-800-656-4673)

Yellow Ribbon Foundation (Suicide Prevention):
www.yellowribbon.org

SHARE WITH US

We hope that *Chicken Soup for the Soul Presents Teens Talkin' Faith* has touched your heart and inspired your soul. We believe that God was present throughout the writing of this book, and that He is present with you now. Please turn to Him for guidance; rely on Him for hope. You are surely worth His love!

We wrote and compiled this book because we believed that it would make a difference in your life. Our prayer was that this book would renew and reinforce your established faith or help lead you to a new and everlasting relationship with God. If *Teens Talkin' Faith* has affected you in such a way, we would love to hear about it! Please write via our website, www.teenstalkinfaith.com, and tell us how this book impacted you.

Also, if you are interested in contributing your perspective to any of our upcoming books, we would be pleased to accept your submission. Please peruse our website, www.chickensoup.com, to see what we are working on.

Thank you and God bless!

SUPPORTING OTHERS

PARTNERSHIP OF COMMUNITY RESOURCES

The Partnership of Community Resources provides a network of citizens, businesses, and agencies for cooperation, planning, and interaction to maximize resources and address the changing needs of our community through substance-abuse prevention and wellness promotion.

The goal at the Partnership of Community Resources is simple: extraordinary customer service as we provide our customer's needs in leadership and advocacy of PREVENTION. Chicken Soup for the Soul has chosen the Partnership as their charity of choice because the majority of Michelle Trujillo's years in education have been dedicated to helping teenagers to make healthy choices. The Partnership provides resources and programs in her community that support and promote her philosophy with teens. Their programs support prevention for teens in the areas of drug, alcohol, and tobacco use, teen pregnancy, and suicide.

Partnership of Community Resources
1528 Highway 395 N, Suite 100
Gardnerville, NV 89410
(775) 782-8611
www.partnership-resource.org

WHO IS JACK CANFIELD?

Jack Canfield is the cocreator and editor of the Chicken Soup for the Soul series, which *Time* magazine has called "the publishing phenomenon of the decade." The series now has 105 titles with over 100 million copies in print in forty-one languages. Jack is also the coauthor of eight other bestselling books, including *The Success Principles: How to Get from Where You Are to Where You Want to Be; Dare to Win; The Aladdin Factor; You've Got to Read This Book;* and *The Power of Focus: How to Hit Your Business and Personal and Financial Targets with Absolute Certainty.*

Jack has recently developed a telephone coaching program and an online coaching program based on his most recent book, *The Success Principles.* He also offers a seven-day Breakthrough to Success seminar every summer, which attracts 400 people from fifteen countries around the world.

Jack has conducted intensive personal and professional development seminars on the principles of success for over 900,000 people in twenty-one countries around the world. He has spoken to hundreds of thousands of others at numerous conferences and conventions and has been seen by millions of viewers on national television shows such as *The Today Show, Fox and Friends, Inside Edition, Hard Copy,* CNN's *Talk Back Live, 20/20, Eye to Eye,* the NBC *Nightly News,* and the CBS *Evening News.*

Jack is the recipient of many awards and honors, including three honorary doctorates and a Guinness World Records Certificate for having seven books from the Chicken Soup for the Soul series appearing on the *New York Times* bestseller list on May 24, 1998.

To write to Jack or for inquiries about Jack as a speaker, his coaching programs, or his seminars, use the following contact information:

The Canfield Companies
P.O. Box 30880 • Santa Barbara, CA 93130
Phone: 805-563-2935 • Fax: 805-563-2945
E-mail: info@jackcanfield.com
Website: www.jackcanfield.com

WHO IS MARK VICTOR HANSEN?

In the area of human potential, no one is more respected than Mark Victor Hansen. For more than thirty years, Mark has focused solely on helping people from all walks of life reshape their personal vision of what's possible. His powerful messages of possibility, opportunity, and action have created powerful change in thousands of organizations and millions of individuals worldwide.

He is a sought-after keynote speaker, bestselling author, and marketing maven. Mark's credentials include a lifetime of entrepreneurial success and an extensive academic background. He is a prolific writer with many bestselling books, such as *The One-Minute Millionaire, Cracking the Millionaire Code, How to Make the Rest of Your Life the Best of Your Life, The Power of Focus, The Aladdin Factor,* and *Dare to Win,* in addition to the Chicken Soup for the Soul series. Mark has made a profound influence through his library of audios, videos, and articles in the areas of big thinking, sales achievement, wealth building, publishing success, and personal and professional development.

Mark is the founder of the MEGA Seminar Series. MEGA Book Marketing University and Building Your MEGA Speaking Empire are annual conferences where Mark coaches and teaches new and aspiring authors, speakers, and experts on building lucrative publishing and speaking careers. Other MEGA events include MEGA Info-Marketing and My MEGA Life.

As a philanthropist and humanitarian, Mark works tirelessly for organizations such as Habitat for Humanity, American Red Cross, March of Dimes, Childhelp USA, and many others. He is the recipient of numerous awards that honor his entrepreneurial spirit, philanthropic heart, and business acumen. He is a lifetime member of the Horatio Alger Association of Distinguished Americans, an organization that honored Mark with the prestigious Horatio Alger Award for his extraordinary life achievements.

Mark Victor Hansen is an enthusiastic crusader of what's possible and is driven to make the world a better place.

Mark Victor Hansen & Associates, Inc.
P.O. Box 7665 • Newport Beach, CA 92658
Phone: 949-764-2640 • Fax: 949-722-6912
Website: www.markvictorhansen.com

WHO IS MICHELLE L. TRUJILLO?

When it comes to teenagers, no one knows them or loves them like Mrs. T! As a health and alternative education teacher, youth group leader, and inspirational speaker, Michelle shares her enthusiasm, faith, and energy with young people as she challenges them to make healthy choices. She is a rare commodity as an expert in the field of teens, teen-parent communication, and teen decision-making because her talents extend beyond research expertise and touch the hearts of teenagers, their parents, and their teachers on a daily basis.

Michelle's experience is vast. A former Teacher of the Year and a four-time selection to Who's Who Among American Teachers, Michelle has appeared on television (including *Oprah*) and radio across the nation as a guest expert on teenagers. She has designed site-based peer education curricula and facilitated Student Assistance Programs. In addition, Michelle is the founder of an Alternative Education Program called F.O.C.U.S. The acronym represents Found Our Chance to Unlock Success, and the program exemplifies Michelle's ambition to guide teens to make choices based on faith and character.

Michelle's first book, *Why Can't We Talk? What Teens Would Share if Parents Would Listen,* was an Editor's Choice selection in *Teen People Magazine* and has appealed to both teens and their parents. You can find out more about *Why Can't We Talk?* or submit stories for future publications at www.teenstalkinfaith.com. You can also share your thoughts with Mrs. T at Mrs.t@teenstalkinfaith.com.

MORE IN THE SERIES

Code #2556 • $14.95

Code #4079 • $14.95

Chicken Soup African American Soul
Chicken Soup African American Woman's Soul
Chicken Soup Breast Cancer Survivor's Soul
Chicken Soup Bride's Soul
Chicken Soup Caregiver's Soul
Chicken Soup Cat Lover's Soul
Chicken Soup Christian Family Soul
Chicken Soup College Soul
Chicken Soup Couple's Soul
Chicken Soup Dieter's Soul
Chicken Soup Dog Lover's Soul
Chicken Soup Entrepreneur's Soul
Chicken Soup Expectant Mother's Soul
Chicken Soup Father's Soul
Chicken Soup Fisherman's Soul
Chicken Soup Girlfriend's Soul
Chicken Soup Golden Soul
Chicken Soup Golfer's Soul, Vol. I, II
Chicken Soup Horse Lover's Soul, Vol. I, II
Chicken Soup Inspire a Woman's Soul
Chicken Soup Kid's Soul, Vol. I, II
Chicken Soup Mother's Soul, Vol. I, II
Chicken Soup Parent's Soul
Chicken Soup Pet Lover's Soul
Chicken Soup Preteen Soul, Vol. I, II
Chicken Soup Scrapbooker's Soul
Chicken Soup Sister's Soul, Vol. I, II
Chicken Soup Shopper's
Chicken Soup Soul, Vol. I-VI
Chicken Soup at Work
Chicken Soup Sports Fan's Soul
Chicken Soup Teenage Soul, Vol. I-IV
Chicken Soup Woman's Soul, Vol. I, II

To order direct: Telephone (800) 441-5569 • www.hcibooks.com
Prices do not include shipping and handling. Your response code is CCS.